KATYAYANA AND PATANJALI

THEIR

RELATION TO EACH OTHER,

AND TO

PANINI.

KATYAYANA AND PATANJALI
THEIR
RELATION TO EACH OTHER,
AND TO
PANINI.

BY

F. KIELHORN, PH. D.,
PROFESSOR OF ORIENTAL LANGUAGES, DECCAN COLLEGE, POONA.

GYAN

Published by

GYAN

Gyan Publishing House
5, Ansari Road
Daryaganj, New Delhi-110002
Phone: 011-47034999, 9811692060
E-mail: books@gyanbooks.com

Distribution Network
gyanbooks.com
India, USA, Canada, UK, Australia, France

ISBN : 978-81-212-2568-7 (HB)
First Published, 1876

2nd Impression 2021

Printed at: Gyan Press, Delhi.

Katyayana and Patanjali their Relation to Each other and to Panini
Author: F. Kielhorn

KÂTYÂYANA AND PATANJALI:

THEIR

RELATION TO EACH OTHER,

AND TO

PÂNINI.

BY

F. KIELHORN, Ph. D.,

PROFESSOR OF ORIENTAL LANGUAGES, DECCAN COLLEGE, POONA.

Bombay:

PRINTED AT THE

EDUCATION SOCIETY'S PRESS, BYCULLA.

1876.

CONTENTS.

KÂTYÂYANA AND PATANJALI:

THEIR RELATION TO EACH OTHER AND TO PÂNINI.

I.

AMONG all the European scholars who have been engaged in the study of the works of the Sanskṛit grammarians, no one has more patiently, minutely, and thoroughly examined the Mahâbhâshya, than the late Prof. Goldstücker. His essay on Pâṇini betrays a familiarity with the work of Patanjali to which no other scholar has as yet attained, and which few are likely to acquire in the future. It is on this account that the views which have been expressed by Prof. Goldstücker regarding the Mahâbhâshya, are deserving of the highest consideration; but the very weight which justly attaches to that scholar's opinions, at the same time imposes on those who may devote themselves to grammatical studies after him, the duty of independently examining and testing their value, and of publicly discussing such doubts and objections as may occur to them in the course of their own reading. And the adoption of such a course appears to be the more called for, when we find that not only have some of the views held by Prof. Goldstücker been apparently widely adopted without such examination, but that views have even been ascribed to him which are at variance with those to which he has actually given expression in his 'Pâṇini.'

In an article on the Mahâbhâshya published in the *Indian Antiquary,* vol. V., page 241, I ventured to express some doubts as to whether the nature and the object of the Vârttikas of Kâtyâyana and of the Mahâbhâshya of Patanjali had been correctly described by other scholars. I would gladly have deferred discussion on this point to the time when I might have been enabled to subject the whole of the Mahâbhâshya to a thorough and searching examination; but having been led publicly to question the accuracy of others, I feel bound to lay before the reader such objections to the current views regarding the works of Kâtyâyana and Patanjali, as have led me to doubt their correctness.

On pp. 119—121 of his essay on Pâṇini, Prof. Goldstücker has described the nature and the object of the Vârttikas of Kâtyâyana and of the work of Patanjali in the following paragraphs:—

'"The characteristic feature of a Vârttika," says Nâgojibhaṭṭa, "is criticism in regard to that which is omitted or imperfectly expressed in a Sûtra." (*Note:* Nâgojibhaṭṭa on Kaiyyaṭa . . . . . वार्त्तिकमिति । सूत्रेऽनुक्तदुरुक्तचिन्ताकरत्वं वार्त्तिकत्वम्). A Vârttika of Kâtyâyana is therefore not a commentary which explains, but an animadversion which completes. In proposing to himself to write Vârttikas on Pâṇini, Kâtyâyana did not mean to justify and to defend the rules of Pâṇini, but to find fault with them; and whoever has gone through his work must avow that he has done so to his heart's content' . . . . . . 'Kâtyâyana, in short, does not leave the impression of an admirer or friend of Pâṇini, but that of an antagonist,—often, too, of an unfair antagonist' . . . . .

'The position of Patanjali is analogous, though not identical. Far from being a commentator on Pâṇini, he also could more properly be called an author of Vârttikas. But as he has two predecessors to deal with instead of one—and two predecessors, too, one of whom is an adversary of the other,—his Great Commentary undergoes, of necessity, the influence of the double task he has to perform, now of criticising Pâṇini and then of animadverting upon Kâtyâyana. Therefore, in order to show where he coincided with, or where he differed from, the criticisms of Kâtyâyana, he had to write a comment on the Vârttikas of this latter grammarian; and thus the Mahâbhâshya became not only a commentary in the ordinary sense of the word, but also, as the case might be, a critical discussion, *on the Vârttikas of Kâtyâyana*; while its *Ishṭis*, on the other hand, are original Vârttikas on such Sûtras of Pâṇini as called for his own remarks.'

'I have already mentioned that Patanjali often refutes the strictures of Kâtyâyana and takes the part of Pâṇini' . . . . . .

'His object being, like that of Kâtyâyana, merely a critical one, Patanjali comments upon the Vârttikas of Kâtyâyana, because such a comment of his implies, of necessity, criticisms, either on Pâṇini or on Kâtyâyana; and, in consequence, no Vârttika could be left unnoticed by him. Again, independently of Kâtyâyana, he writes his own Vârttikas to Sûtras not sufficiently or not at all animadverted upon by the latter grammarian, because they, too, are criticisms, viz. on Pâṇini.'

Prof. Weber, in his article on the Mahâbhâshya (*Indische Studien*, vol. XIII.) has adopted Prof. Goldstücker's view regarding the nature of Kâtyâyana's Vârttikas, but to the same scholar's remarks on the work of Patanjali he appears to have given a meaning, against which Prof. Goldstücker would seem to have distinctly and repeatedly guarded himself. On page 297 Prof. Weber writes:—

'Through Goldstücker . . . . we then learnt that Patanjali behaves much less like a commentator on Pâṇini than like a defender of the latter against the unjust attacks of Kâtyâyana, the author of the Vârttikas. And this view is indeed fully borne out by appearances.'

On page 298 Prof. Weber speaks of Kâtyâyana as attacking or combating the Sûtras of Pâṇini, and of Patanjali as refuting the Vârttikas of Kâtyâyana.

On page 321 Prof. Weber says:—

'The red thread which runs through the work (*i.e.* the Mahâbhâshya) is—and on this Goldstücker was the first to lay particular stress—the polemic against the Vârttikakâra;' and on the same page he speaks of the Sûtras as attacked by Kâtyâyana.

On page 399 Prof. Weber writes: 'He (*i.e.* Kâtyâyana) it is to combat whom is the special object of the Bhâshya;' and he tells us that the Bhâshya contains the Vârttikas 'together with their refutation' by Patanjali.

Finally, on page 502 Prof. Weber asks: 'What business have Kâtyâyana's Vârttikas, whose object it surely is to attack Pâṇini's Sûtras, in the introduction of the Bhâshya?'

While, then, according to Prof. Goldstücker, Patanjali commented on the Vârttikas of Kâtyâyana in order to show *where he coincided with, or where he differed from,* the criticisms of that grammarian, frequently attaching, at the same time, to quote another passage from the essay on Pâṇini, 'his own critical remarks to the emendations of Kâtyâyana, *often in support of the views of the latter,*' Prof. Weber maintains, apparently on the authority of Prof. Goldstücker, that the Vârttikas of Kâtyâyana have been *refuted* by Patanjali. And Prof. Weber is not the only scholar who has given this meaning to Prof. Goldstücker's words. For Dr. Burnell in his essay *On the Aindra School,* likewise describes the relation to each other of Kâtyâyana and Patanjali in the following terms (page 91) 'Kâtyâyana criticised Pâṇini, and Patanjali replied in justification of the latter,' (and on page 92) 'the Mahâbhâshya is . . . a skilful compilation of the views of Pâṇini's critics and of their refutation by Patanjali.'

Setting aside for the present the work of Patanjali, it would appear from the above quotations, that Prof. Goldstücker and Prof. Weber are agreed in regarding Kâtyâyana as an antagonist or, to speak more accurately, as an unfair antagonist of Pâṇini, and that both these scholars are of opinion that Kâtyâyana had no other motive in composing the Vârttikas than to attack, or to find fault with, the Sûtras of his predecessor. If we try to examine how far this view of the literary activity of Kâtyâyana may be correct, we meet at the very outset of our enquiry with the difficulty that neither Prof. Goldstücker nor Prof. Weber has furnished us with a test by which to recognise the Vârttikas of Kâtyâyana, that neither scholar has shown to us a way of reconstructing out of the Mahâbhâshya, as we find it in our MSS, the work of Kâtyâyana as it must have existed before it was by Patanjali embodied in his own work. And not only have both withheld from us their guidance in deciding this most important and fundamental question, but they have incidentally ventured on statements the adoption of which, in my opinion, would be sure to mislead, and have in individual cases expressed opinions opposed to those which are unanimously held by the native grammarians.

It is true Prof. Goldstücker commences his description of the nature and the object of Kâtyâyana's Vârttikas with Nâgojîbhaṭṭa's definition of the term वार्त्तिक, but it must be apparent that that definition, even supposing it to have been rightly understood, can be of but little value in determining what are *Kâtyâyana's* Vârttikas, for we find it stated by Prof. Goldstücker that the Mahâbhâshya contains not only Kâtyâyana's Vârttikas, but also Vârttikas of Patanjali. Moreover, no reader of the essay on Pâṇini can fail to perceive that practically Prof. Goldstücker has little heeded Nâgojîbhaṭṭa's definition, and that he frequently, and I may add, correctly, has prefixed the words *Vârttika* or *Kâtyâyana* to remarks which justify and teach the proper application of, without in any way taking exception to, the Sûtras to which they refer. Turning to incidental notices, we find that in a note on page 29 Prof. Goldstücker speaks of the usual addition of Kâtyâyana इति वक्तव्यम्; in reality this phrase appears to be entirely foreign to the style of Kâtyâyana, and occurs either in the original remarks of Patanjali, or in the explanations given by this scholar of Kâtyâyana's Vârttikas. Nor is another statement (in a note on page 23) that '*Kâtyâyana never* gives *instances*' less liable to objection, for there *are* Vârttikas, on P. I, 1, 39 and other rules, which lay down general rules and at the same time *give instances*.

Prof. Weber has adopted Prof. Goldstücker's rendering of the definition of the term Vârttika, and on the strength of that definition so understood, he apparently is inclined to deny, that Vârttikas occur in the first Âhnika of the Mahâbhâshya, *viz.*, because no Sûtras of Pâṇini's are treated of in that Âhnika, and because therefore there is as yet no occasion for finding fault with Pâṇini. Though I have found reason to admire their thorough knowledge of the Mahâbhâshya, I am by no means inclined to assert that men like Kaiyaṭa, Bhaṭṭojídîkshita, and Nâgojîbhaṭṭa are free from error. But when I see that those scholars unanimously call certain statements which we meet with in the first Âhnika, by the name Vârttika, while at the same time they adhere to the current definition of that term as recorded by Nâgojibhaṭṭa, I in the first instance feel strongly moved to question whether the force of that definition has been rightly apprehended by Prof. Goldstücker. And when Prof. Weber *justifies* his doubts as to whether the words यथा लौकिकवैदिकेषु in the first Âhnika are part of a Vârttika, by stating that the same words in other passages in which they occur (*viz.* on pages 28*b*, 45*a*, 136*b* of the first volume of the Lith. Ben. Edn., and on P. VI, 1, 84) are *certainly not* Vârttikas, I can only reply that the sentence ending with यथा लौकिकवैदिकेषु on page 28*b is* called a Vârttika by Kaiyaṭa, and that I consider those words as part of Vârttikas in the remaining passages also. On page 399 *(Ind. Stud. XIII.)* Prof. Weber states that *on the whole* the Vârttikas of Kâtyâyana are easily detected in the Mahâbhâshya, because *as a rule* they are followed by a short paraphrase which ends with the word वक्तव्य or कर्तव्य. This would seem to be an improvement on Prof. Goldstücker's remark concerning इति वक्तव्यम्, but it contains no test by which to recognize all the Vârttikas of Kâtyâyana or even most of them; nor did Prof. Weber *intend* to lay down a general rule. Moreover, Prof. Weber, too, has regarded as Vârttikas statements of Patanjali which end with इति वक्तव्यम्.

So far as we know at present, the Vârttikas of Kâtyâyana do not exist separately in MS. MSS. which profess to give the Śrîmadbhagavat-Kâtyâyanavirachita-vârttikapâṭha are indeed to be met with in different and widely distant parts of India,* but a very superficial examination is sufficient to prove that the Vârtikapâṭha which they contain, has been compiled and, I have no

* A so-called *Vârtikapâṭhaḥ* has also been printed at Benares.

hesitation in saying, very carelessly compiled from the Mahâbhâshya at a comparatively modern date. Nor do the commentators on the Mahâbhâshya, or other scholars who have written on Pâṇini, render us any very great assistance in reconstructing the work of Kâtyâyana, for they only occasionally contrast the views of Patanjali with those of the Vârttikakâra, and they tell us only incidentally that a particular statement is a Vârttika or belongs to Kâtyâyana. And Patanjali himself, the author of the Great Commentary, is even more reticent.

In attempting then to determine which are the Vârttikas of Kâtyâyana, we are mainly left to our own resources. Given the Mahâbhâshya, which in accordance with the tradition handed down to us and to judge from incidental remarks that occur in the work itself, contains both Vârttikas of Kâtyâyana and original matter contributed by Patanjali, we must attempt to find out whether there is anything in the method and the style of the work that would enable us to separate the former from the latter. In making an attempt of this nature, we may avail ourselves of the assistance rendered to us by the later native grammarians—not indeed on account of any traditional knowledge, which they may or may not have been possessed of, but because they evince a familiarity with the work of Patanjali in which they will never again be equalled,—and if the result to which our enquiry may lead should happen to coincide with their views, such accordance will tend to assure us that our attempt has not been entirely vain or fruitless. In this spirit and from this point of view I have examined that portion of the Mahâbhâshya which treats of the rules in the first Pâda of Pâṇini's grammar; the results which I have arrived at in the course of that examination I have tested by applying them in the later portions, and having found them confirmed, I now submit them to the judgment of others.

II.

The first thing sure to arrest the attention of the student of the Mahâbhâshya, is in my opinion this, that the method of discussion followed in it, is distinctly two-fold. If we examine that part of the work which treats of the rules in the first Pâda of the Ashṭâdhyâyî, we find that in the case of some rules the discussion is begun, continued, and ended in a series of short epigrammatic sentences. The paraphrases which invariably accompany these sentences, and the explanatory remarks which are sometimes added, form no integral part of the discussion. They facilitate the understanding of the sentences to which they are attached; but an intelligent reader might supply them for himself. They contribute nothing to the discussion of which at first sight they seem to form a part.

On the other hand, there are other rules in the discussion of which such short sentences accompanied by paraphrase and explanatory remarks, are completely wanting. Wherever this is the case, every part of the discussion is essentially necessary, and nothing could have been omitted without either breaking the continuity of the discussion, or depriving the student of information which no mere exegetical ability of his could have supplied him with.

As instances of rules where the former method has been exclusively adopted I cite P. I, 1, 10, 48, 54, 60, and 71; as instances for the latter P. I, 1, 14, 25, 28, 30, 32, 35, 37, 55, 74 and 75.

On P. I, 1, 10 all essential points of the discussion are contained in the following sentences:—

(*a*) अज्झलोः प्रतिषेधे शकारप्रतिषेधोऽज्झल्त्वात् ।

(*b*) तत्र सवर्णलोपे दोषः ।

(*c*) सिद्धमनच्त्वात् ।

(*d*) वाक्यापरिसमाप्तेर्वा ॥

On P. I, 1, 48 in the following:—

(*a*) एच इग्वचनं सवर्णाकारनिवृत्त्यर्थम् ।

(*b*) दीर्घप्रसङ्गस्तु निवर्तकत्वात् ।

(*c*) सिद्धमेङः सस्थानत्वात् ।

(*d*) ऐचोश्चोत्तरभूयस्त्वात् ॥

On P. I, 1, 54 in the following single sentence:—

अलोऽन्त्यस्यादेः परस्यानेकाल्शित्सर्वस्येत्यपवादविप्रतिषेधात्सर्वादेशः ॥

On P. I, 1, 60 in the following sentences:—

(*a*) लोपसंज्ञायामर्थसतोरुक्तम् ।

(*b*) सर्वप्रसङ्गस्तु सर्वस्यान्यत्रादृष्टत्वात् ।

(*c*) तत्र प्रत्ययलक्षणप्रतिषेधः ।

(*d*) सिद्धं तु प्रसक्तादर्शनस्य लोपसंज्ञत्वात् ॥

On P. I, 1, 71 in the following:—

(*a*) आदिरन्त्येन सहेतेत्यसंप्रत्ययः संज्ञिनोऽनिर्देशात् ।

(*b*) सिद्धं त्वादिरिता सह तन्मध्यस्येति वचनात् ।

(*c*) संबन्धिशब्दैर्वा तुल्यम् ॥

I select the discussion on this last rule as an instance to show that all that has been stated regarding that rule of Pâṇini's in the Mahâbhâshya is really contained in the three sentences which I have pointed out, and that what we find besides is paraphrase and explanatory remark. The whole Bhâshya on P. I, 1, 71 आदिरन्त्येन सहेता runs thus:—

आदिरन्त्येन सहेतेत्यसंप्रत्ययः संज्ञिनोऽनिर्देशात् ॥

आदिरन्त्येन सहेतेत्यसंप्रत्ययः । किं कारणम् । संज्ञिनोऽनिर्देशात् । न हि संज्ञिनो निर्दिश्यन्ते ॥

सिद्धं त्वादिरिता सह तन्मध्यस्येति वचनात् ॥

सिद्धमेतत् । कथम् । आदिरन्त्येन सहेता गृह्यमाणः स्वस्य च रूपस्य ग्राहकस्तन्मध्यानां चेति वक्तव्यम् ॥

संबन्धिशब्दैर्वा तुल्यम् ॥

संबन्धिशब्दैर्वा तुल्यमेतत् । तद्यथा । मातरि वर्तितव्यं पितरि शुश्रूषितव्यमिति । न चोच्यते स्वस्यां मातरि स्वस्मिन्पितरीति संबन्धाच्च गम्यते या यस्य माता यश्च यस्य पितेति । एवमिहाप्या-

2

दिरन्त्य इति संबन्धिशब्दावेतौ । तत्र संबन्धादेतद्गन्तव्यं यं प्रति य आदिरन्त्य इति च भवति तस्य ग्रहणं भवति स्वस्य च रूपस्येति ॥

To show how this method differs from that which has been followed on P. I, 1,14 and the other rules enumerated above, in the discussion on which we meet with no sentences that are accompanied by paraphrase and explanatory remarks, I cite for the sake of brevity the Bhâshya on P. I, 1, 25 and 30.

P. I, 1, 25:—डति च ॥ इदं डतिग्रहणं द्विः क्रियते संख्यासंज्ञायां षट्संज्ञायां च । एकं शक्यमकर्तुम् । कथम् । यदि तावत्संख्यासंज्ञायां क्रियते षट्संज्ञायां न करिष्यते । कथम् । ष्णान्ता षडित्यत्र डतीत्यनुवर्तिष्यते । अथ षट्संज्ञायां क्रियते संख्यासंज्ञायां न करिष्यते । डति चेत्यत्र संख्यासंज्ञाप्यनुवर्तिष्यते ॥

P. I, 1, 30:—तृतीयासमासे ॥ समास इति वर्तमाने पुनः समासग्रहणं किमर्थम् । अयं तृतीयासमासोऽस्त्येव प्राथमकल्पिको यस्मिन्नैकपद्यमैकस्वर्यमेकविभक्तित्वं चेति । अस्ति च तादर्थ्यात्ताच्छब्द्यं तृतीयासमासार्थानि पदानि तृतीयासमास इति । तद्यत्तादर्थ्यात्ताच्छब्द्यं तस्येदं ग्रहणम् ॥ अथवा समास इति वर्तमाने पुनः समासग्रहणस्यैतत्प्रयोजनं योगाङ्गं यथा विज्ञायेत । सति च योगाङ्गे योगविभागः करिष्यते । तृतीया । तृतीयासमासे सर्वादीनि सर्वनामसंज्ञानि न भवन्ति । मासपूर्वाय देहि संवत्सरपूर्वाय देहि । ततोऽसमासे । असमासे च तृतीयायाः सर्वादीनि सर्वनामसंज्ञानि न भवन्ति । मासेन पूर्वाय देहि संवत्सरेण पूर्वाय देहीति ॥

If we now ask whether there is anything in the nature or in the object of the remarks on the two sets of rules cited above which could have induced the author of the Mahâbhâshya to adopt two distinctly different methods of discussion, we are bound to answer in the negative. For the object of the discussions on P. I, 1, 10, &c., is no other than that of the discussions on P. I, 1, 14, &c., either to defend Pâṇini against objections which might be raised or have actually been raised, or to show the real meaning and the scope of his rules, or to prove that a particular rule need not have been given, &c. Nor is it the extent of the remarks appended to P. I, 1, 10, &c. that could have induced Patanjali to sum up, as it were, the discussion in a few short sentences, which, it might be argued, are more easily remembered by the student than long discussions void of such summary sentences ; for the remarks attached to some of the rules contained in the second set are even more lengthy than those attached to some rules of the first set.

Now I am well aware of the fact that there have lived authors in India who have furnished us with commentaries on works composed by themselves, and if Patanjali had carried on his discussions on Pâṇini's rules throughout his whole work in the manner which he follows, *e.g.* on P. I, 1, 10, I would admit the possibility of his belonging to that class of authors. But it appears to me extremely unlikely that the same scholar in the composition of one and the same work should, for no discernible reason whatsoever, have followed two methods of discussion so different as those which Patanjali would seem to have adopted in the Mahâbhâshya, and the only way in which I am able to account for such an apparent inconsistency is by assuming that in the discussions on P. I, 1, 10, &c., Patanjali has simply paraphrased and commented on the words of another scholar, while in those on P. I, 1, 14, &c. he has given us his own original remarks on Pâṇini's Sûtras. In other words, I would venture to assume that those short sentences on P. I, 1, 10, &c., by means of which the discussion is carried on from beginning to end, and which we find paraphrased and explained in the Mahâbhâshya, are not of Patanjali's own authorship, but form part of the work of another scholar on which, in these instances, the author of the Mahâbhâshya is merely commenting. And this assumption is rendered the more probable when we find that the author of the Mahâbhâshya in the discussion on one of the rules which I have instanced above, on P. I, 1, 10, does not merely give us his own interpretation of the sentences अज्झलौ : प्रतिषेधे चाकारमविशेषो

ऽप्रसक्तत्वात् &c., but also quotes, after having done so, the interpretation by another (अपर) of the very same sentences, which interpretation, in some respects, materially differs from his own. Such a proceeding of his would, in my opinion, be altogether inexplicable, were the sentences अज्झलोः प्रतिषेधे, &c. of Patanjali's own authorship. Of *whose* authorship they are, I will not at present stop to enquire. I content myself with stating that the sentences *(a)* and *(b)* on P. I, 1, 10 are called *Vârttika* by Bhaṭṭojidîkshita in his Śabdakaustubha, that *(c)* and *(d)* on the same rule are ascribed to the *Vârttikakâra* by the same scholar, and that the sentence *(b)* on P. I, 1, 71 is called a *Vârttika* by Nâgojîbhaṭṭa in his Pratyâkhyânasaṃgraha. On the other hand, the most diligent search has not enabled me to discover in the works of the commentators an indication that they have regarded any part of the discussions on P. I, 1, 14 &c. as Vârttika, or have ascribed any portion of them to the Vârttikakâra. On the contrary, Kaiyaṭa* distinctly ascribes the statement which we find on P. I,

* That Kaiyaṭa is older than the Kâśikâ-vṛitti appears to be by no means so certain as has been generally assumed to be the case. For in his gloss on P. I, 1, 75 and elsewhere Kaiyaṭa would seem distinctly to quote from the Kâśikâ. Nor is it at all certain that the name of the author of the Kâśikâ-vṛitti was *Vâmana Jayâditya*. On the contrary, it clearly follows from a remark of Bhaṭṭojidîkshita's in his Śabdakaustubha, that the Kâśikâ-vṛitti is the work of the *two* scholars Jayâditya *and* Vâmana; that it was begun by the former and concluded by the latter. On page 122*a* of my MS. of the Śabdakaustubha Bhaṭṭojidîkshita writes as follows:—

तथा च ग्लाजिस्थेति सूत्रे (III, 2, 139) श्लोकवार्त्तिकम् । क्स्नोर्गित्त्वान्न . . . कगोरितोरिति ॥ जयादित्योऽप्येवम् ॥ वामनस्तु ग्लाजिस्थश्चेत्यत्र स्था आ इत्याकारं प्रश्लिष्य क्स्नुप्रत्ययान्तस्य तिष्ठतेराकार एव न त्वीत्वमिति व्याख्यानादेव स्थास्नोः सिद्धौ न कापि गकारप्रश्लेषः कार्य इत्याह ॥

Jayâditya's view is that given in the Kâśikâ on III, 2, 139; and that view is distinctly refuted, as stated by Bhaṭṭojidîkshita, by Vâmana in the same Kâśikâ on P. VII, 2, 11 (केचिदत्र द्विककारकनिर्देशेन गकारप्रश्लेषं वर्णयन्तीत्यादि). It is impossible that the author of the comment on VII, 2, 11 should be the same person who composed the comment on III, 2, 139. It will, I think, be possible to show approximately where Jayâditya's portion of the work ends and where Vâmana's begins.

I, 75, to the *Bhâshyakâra*, notwithstanding the fact that it ends with the phrase इति वक्तव्यम्.

The number of rules in the discussion of which either of the two methods described in the above has been exclusively adopted, appears small and insignificant, when it is compared with the number of those rules in discussing which the author of the Mahâbhâshya would seem to have employed both methods, one by the side of the other. In the case of some rules the discussion opens with one or more paraphrased sentences, while it concludes with remarks in which such sentences are wanting; or on the other hand it opens with remarks that contain no such sentences, and it is carried on and concluded by means of paraphrased sentences. Again, there are numerous rules where both methods are continually changing places with each other.

On P. I, I, 45 the discussion opens with the paraphrased sentences:

(*a*) संप्रसारणसंज्ञायां वाक्यस्य संज्ञा चेद्वर्णविधिः ।

(*b*) वर्णसंज्ञा चेन्निर्वृत्तिः ।

(*c*) विभक्तिविशेषनिर्देशस्तु ज्ञापक उभयसंज्ञात्वस्य ।

and it concludes with remarks that contain no paraphrased sentences, but the object of which is identical with that of the paraphrased sentence *(c)*, *viz.* to defend Pâṇini's rule from the objections raised to it in *(a)* and *(b)*.

On P. I, I, 6 the discussion opens with the paraphrased sentences:

(*a*) दीधीवेव्योश्छन्दोविषयत्वाद्दृष्टानुविधित्वाच्च छन्दसोऽदीधेदवीधयुरिति गुणदर्शनादप्रतिषेधः ।

(*b*) दीध्यदिति च इयन्व्यत्ययेन ।

which are intended to show that दीधीवेवी might have been omitted from Pâṇini's rule; and it concludes with remarks in which no paraphrased sentence occurs, but the purport of which is similar to that of *(a)* and *(b)*, *viz.* to prove that इट् might have been omitted likewise.

On P. I, 1, 11 the discussion opens with lengthy remarks which consider the propriety of the Anubandha त् of the terms ईत् &c. of Pâṇini's rule, remarks in which we do not meet with any paraphrased sentences; and it is continued by means of the following paraphrased sentences which consider the several possible interpretations of Pâṇini's rule :—

(*a*) ईदादयो यद्द्विवचनं प्रगृह्या इति चेदन्त्यस्य विधिः ।

(*b*) ईदाद्यन्तं यद्द्विवचनमिति चेदेकस्य विधिः ।

(*c*) न वाद्यन्तवत्त्वात् ।

(*d*) ईदाद्यन्तं यद्द्विवचनान्तमिति चेल्लुकि प्रतिषेधः ।

(*e*) सप्तम्यामर्थग्रहणं ज्ञापकं प्रत्ययलक्षणप्रतिषेधस्य ।

On P. I, 1, 49 the discussion opens with remarks on the term स्थानेयोगा; it is carried on by means of the paraphrased sentences :

(*a*) षष्ठीस्थानेयोगवचनं नियमार्थम् ।

(*b*) अवयवषष्ठ्यादिष्वतिप्रसङ्गः शासो गोह इति ।

(*c*) अवयवषष्ठ्यादीनां चाप्राप्तिर्योगस्यासंदिग्धत्वात् ।

the purport of which is to show the object of Pâṇini's rule, to state an objection to which it is liable, and to refute that objection; (*c*) is followed by remarks without paraphrase, identical in purpose with (*c*); those remarks are in turn followed by the paraphrased sentence :

(*d*) विशिष्टा वा षष्ठी स्थानेयोगा ।

which suggests a different way of obviating the objection raised in (*b*); and after that the discussion is wound up with remarks in which no paraphrased sentences occur, and in which Pâṇini's rule, taken in the sense which is ordinarily ascribed to it, is stated to be superfluous.

And here again we have to observe that there is nothing whatsoever in the nature of the questions discussed, which could seem to have induced the author of the Mahâbhâshya to follow one method in preference to the other, for the remarks which contain no paraphrased sentences are of essentially and identically the same nature as other remarks conveyed to us by means of such sentences, the object of both being either to justify or to find fault with the rules laid down by Pâṇini. We at any rate fail to perceive, why Patanjali on P. I, 1, 11 should have discussed the possible interpretations of that rule (ईदादयो द्विवचनम् or ईदाद्यन्तं द्विवचनम् &c.) in paraphrased and commented sentences, and should not have adopted the same method on P. I, 1, 39 (कृद्यो मान्तः or कृदन्तं मन्मान्तम्) ; or why he should have discussed the propriety of the Anubandha त् of ईत् &c., on P. I, 1, 11 without employing paraphrased sentences, and should, when considering the same question with regard to the Anubandha त् in P. I, 1, 1, have opened the discussion with a paraphrased sentence.

The conclusion to which we are led by these considerations would again seem to be this, that, whenever the author of the Mahâbhâshya in the discussion of Pâṇini's rules makes use of sentences to which he attaches a paraphrase and comment, he, while doing so, is quoting and commenting on the words of another scholar, and that those portions of the discussion which do not consist of paraphrased sentences contain original remarks of Patanjali's, remarks, I may add, which adduce additional evidence in support of, or corrections of, the statements of that other scholar, or discuss questions which had not been raised by him. And there is, I believe, even in that small portion of the Mahâbhâshya on which mainly I have based this enquiry, evidence sufficient to prove that the paraphrased and commented sentences are not of Patanjali's authorship. I have mentioned already that in one instance at least (on P. I, 1, 10) the author of the Mahâbhâshya does not merely give us his own interpretation of the sentences by means of which he carries on the discussion, but also quotes the different interpretation of the very same sentences by another scholar. I may now add a similar instance which occurs in the discussion on P. I, 1, 69. After having paraphrased and commented on the three sentences

सवर्णेऽण्ग्रहणमपरिभाष्यमाकृतिग्रहणात् ।
अनन्यत्वाच्च ।
अनेकान्तो ह्यनन्यत्वकरः ।

Patanjali goes on to say: अपर आह ।

सवर्णेऽण्ग्रहणमपरिभाष्यमाकृतिग्रहणादनन्यत्वम् ।
सवर्णेऽण्ग्रहणमपरिभाष्यम् । आकृतिग्रहणादनन्यत्वं भविष्यति ।
अनन्याकृतिरकारस्याकारस्य च ।
अनेकान्तो ह्यनन्यत्वकरः ।

Here then Patanjali informs us that another scholar has not only given a different interpretation, but has also adopted a different reading, of those very sentences which Patanjali himself has just been making use of. Could we wish for stronger proof that at any rate *these* sentences cannot be Patanjali's own?

Again, after having on P. I, 1, 3 paraphrased the sentence सर्वादेशप्रसङ्गस्त्वनिगन्तस्य in the words सर्वादेशश्च गुणोऽनिगन्तस्य प्राप्नोति, Patanjali shows that *so* understood the sentence would be open to objection, and he therefore proposes another paraphrase and another explanation of the same sentence, which he introduces thus: एवं तर्हि नायं दोषसमुच्चयः । पूर्वापेक्षोऽयं दोषः । ह्यर्थे चायं चः (*i.e.* the च of सर्वादेशश्च) पठितः.—In other words, Patanjali tells us that it would be possible to understand the particle च of the sentence सर्वादेशप्रसङ्गस्त्वनिगन्तस्य either in its ordinary sense or in the sense of हि, and in doing so, and by the manner in which he introduces his second explanation, he, in my opinion, clearly shows that he is commenting on the words of *another*. And the same conclusion we have to draw from another remark of his, on P. I, 1, 63; in which he informs us that the particle च of the paraphrased sentence क्नेर्दीर्घत्वं च does not stand in its proper place, but should have been placed, or should at any rate be understood to stand, immediately after क्नेः (अस्थानेऽयं चः पठितः । क्नेश्च दीर्घत्वम् ।).

I will not try the patience of the reader by adducing many more instances which would all point to the same conclusion, but I cannot refrain from drawing attention to at least two others, because they somewhat differ from those which I have given above. On P. I, 1, 38 the discussion is carried on by means of the following paraphrased sentences:

(*a*) असर्वविभक्तावविभक्तिनिमित्तस्योपसंख्यानम् ।

(*b*) सर्वविभक्त्यविशेषात् ।

(*c*) त्रलादीनां चोपसंख्यानम् ।

(*d*) अविभक्तावितरेतराश्रयत्वादप्रसिद्धिः ।

(*e*) अलिङ्गमसंख्यमिति वा ।

(*f*) सिद्धं तु पाठात् ॥

(*a*—*c*) show that Pâṇini's rule has to be corrected; (*d*) and (*e*) show that two alterations of the rule which might possibly be suggested, can, on account of the objection to which they would be open, and which has been stated in (*d*), not be adopted; (*f*) on the other hand states that the corrections mentioned in (*a*—*c*) need not be made, and that the alterations suggested in (*d*) and (*e*) need not be adopted, as soon as all the Taddhita-affixes intended in Pâṇini's rule are put down in the Gaṇa *svarâdi*. The statement made in (*f*) is opposed to the suggestion made in (*e*), and the particle तु in (*f*) is in its proper place and has its usual force. But if we turn to the paraphrase of (*f*), we find that there तु 'but' has been rendered by वा 'or' (पाठाद्वा सिद्धमेतत्). How are we to account for this rendering? By the simple fact that Patanjali, after commenting on (*e*), has shown that the objection to which the alteration suggested in (*e*) was by the author of the paraphrased sentences considered to be liable, is in reality no objection at all. Patanjali adopts the definition अलिङ्गमसंख्यमव्ययम् which was objected to in (*e*) and for *him* therefore the course indicated in (*f*) is only an *alternative* course. His rendering of तु by वा is inexplicable as long as we consider the paraphrased sentences (*e*) and (*f*) as his own; it admits of a reasonable explanation when we regard them as statements made by another. And that this is the view held by the commentators, follows from Kaiyaṭa's gloss : सिद्धं त्विति । वार्त्तिककारस्यैवेतरेतराश्रयदोषः स्थित एवेति तुशब्दो विशेषप्रदर्शनार्थः । भाष्यकारेण त्वितरेतराश्रयदोषः परिहृत इति वाशब्दार्थस्तुशब्दो व्याख्यातः ।

On P. I, 1, 61 we find the following paraphrased sentences:

(*a*) लुमति प्रत्ययग्रहणमप्रत्ययसंज्ञाप्रतिषेधार्थम् ।

(*b*) प्रयोजनं तद्धितलुकि कंसीयपरशव्ययोर्लुकि च गोप्रकृतिनिवृत्त्यर्थम् ।

(*c*) उक्तं वा ।

(*d*) षष्ठीनिर्देशार्थं तु ।

(*e*) अनिर्देशे हि षष्ठ्यर्थाप्रसिद्धिः ।

(*f*) सर्वादेशार्थं वा वचनप्रामाण्यात् ।

The object of the whole discussion is to prove the necessity of the word प्रत्ययस्य in Pâṇini's rule; one reason for the employment of प्रत्ययस्य is given in (*d-e*), and another *alternative* reason in (*f*). Such being the case, the particle वा in (*f*) would seem to stand in its proper place and to convey the meaning which it usually conveys. But if we again turn to Patanjali's paraphrase of (*f*), we find that he has rendered वा by तर्हि, a word which he elsewhere makes use of to paraphrase the particle तु. The reason for this rendering of his is similar to that for his rendering तु on P. I, 1, 38 by वा. After having commented on (*d-e*), Patanjali has shown that प्रत्ययस्य for the reason stated in (*d-e*) would *not* be necessary; and to *him* therefore (*f*) does not convey an *alternative* reason for the employment of प्रत्ययस्य. In his opinion प्रत्ययस्य is not necessary for the reason given in (*d-e*), *but* it *is* necessary for the reason given in (*f*). His rendering of वा by तर्हि is explained, as soon as and only when we assume that the paraphrased sentences (*d—f*) are not his own but *another's*. And here again we are able to quote Kaiyaṭa in support of the view we have taken; for in commenting on (*f*) that commentator remarks: षष्ठीनिर्देशार्थत्वं तु स्थितमेवेति वार्त्तिककारेण विकल्पार्थो वाशब्दः प्रयुक्तः । . . . भाष्यकारस्तु तदर्थे वाशब्दं व्याचक्षाणः षष्ठीनिर्देशार्थत्वं नेच्छति ।

I have shown in the preceding that the method of discussion followed in the Mahâbhâshya is distinctly twofold; I have attempted to account for this twofold method by assuming that those sentences made use of in the discussion of Pâṇini's rules, which we find to be accompanied by paraphrase and comment, are not of Patanjali's authorship; and I have tried to render this assumption probable by drawing attention to the manner in which those sentences have been paraphrased and commented on in various passages of the Mahâbhâshya. I may be told now that, if then only that portion of the Mahâbhâshya which does not consist of paraphrased sentences were Patanjali's, and if the paraphrased sentences themselves had really to be considered as proceeding from another author, we might well expect that the two parts of the work, being in reality works by different authors, should differ as regards their respective styles and the language employed in either of them. So far from regarding such an objection as hostile to the view which I have ventured to express, I gladly avail myself of it, to adduce the difference of style and of language as additional evidence in favour of the assumption that the paraphrased sentences do not belong to the author of the rest of the Mahâbhâshya. I cannot pretend to undertake at present to show that difference in all its details; all I shall attempt to do here, is to illustrate it by a few characteristic instances.

Very often the question is raised in the Mahâbhâshya whether a particular term employed in Pâṇini's rules conveys one meaning or another, whether we are to understand a rule in one sense or in another, whether a particular term should be understood to be qualified in this or in that way, whether a rule should be regarded as teaching something independently of other rules or as a restrictive rule, &c. In all these cases it is customary to place before the reader both sides of the question and to state the objections to which either side would be liable. And here we have to observe that whenever this is done by means of paraphrased sentences, the particles employed are always चेत् or इति चेत्, and that when it is done without the employment of such sentences the particle used is invariably

यदि, generally followed by अथ. In proof of this I adduce from the paraphrased sentences:

On P. I, 1, 3—(किं पुनरयमलोऽन्त्यशेष आहोस्विदलोऽन्त्यापवादः।.......)

वृद्धिगुणावलोऽन्त्यस्येति चेन्मिदि ..... ग्रहणम्।

इग्मात्रस्येति चेज्जुसि ..... प्रतिषेधः।

On P. I, 1, 11—(कथं पुनरिदं विज्ञायते ....।)

ईदादयो यद्विवचनं प्रगृह्या इति चेदन्त्यस्य विधिः।

ईदाद्यन्तं यद्विवचनमिति चेदेकस्य विधिः।

ईदाद्यन्तं यद्विवचनान्तमिति चेल्लुकि प्रतिषेधः।

On P. I, 1, 45—(किमियं वाक्यस्य संप्रसारणसंज्ञा क्रियते ... आहोस्विद्वर्णस्य।...)

संप्रसारणसंज्ञायां वाक्यस्य संज्ञा चेद्वर्णविधिः।

वर्णसंज्ञा चेन्निर्वृत्तिः।

On P. I, 1, 51—(किमिदमुरण्रपरवचनमन्यनिवृत्त्यर्थम् ... आहोस्विद्रपरत्वमात्रमनेन विधीयते।....)

उरण्रपरवचनमन्यनिवृत्त्यर्थमिति चेदुदात्तादिषु दोषः।

य उः स्थानेऽण् स रपर इति चेद्गुणवृद्ध्योरवर्णाप्रतिपत्तिः।

On P. I, 1, 57—(किं पुनरनन्तरस्य विधिं प्रति स्थानिवद्भाव आहोस्वित्पूर्वमात्रस्य।.....)

अनन्तरस्य चेदेकाननुदात्त ..... वूपसंख्यानम्।

पूर्वमात्रस्येति चेदुपधाह्रस्वत्वम्।

(किं पुनराश्रीयमाणायां प्रकृतौ स्थानिवद्भवत्याहोस्विदविशेषेण।...)

अविशेषेण स्थानिवदिति चेल्लोपयणादेशे गुरुविधिः।

ग्रहणेषु स्थानिवदिति चेज्जग्ध्यादिष्वादेशप्रतिषेधः।

On P. I, 1, 65—(किमिदमल्ग्रहणमन्त्यविशेषणम् ....)

उपधासंज्ञायामल्ग्रहणमन्त्यनिर्देशश्चेत्संघातप्रतिषेधः।

On P. I, 1, 70—(किं पुनरिदं नियमार्थमाहोस्विज्ज्ञापकम् । . .)

तपरस्तत्कालस्येति नियमार्थमिति चेद्दीर्घ० . . . ग्रहणम् ।

ज्ञापकमिति चेद्ध्रस्वग्रहणे दीर्घप्लुतप्रतिषेधः ।

To show how the same or similar questions are discussed when no paraphrases are employed, I instance—

On P. I, 1, 1—(किं पुनरिदं तद्भावितग्रहणम् . . . आहोस्विदादैज्मात्रस्य । . . .)

यदि तद्भावितग्रहणं . . . . न प्राप्नोति ।

अथादैज्मात्रस्य ग्रहणं . . . प्राप्नोति ।

On P. I, 1, 7—(कथमिदं विज्ञायते । . . . .)

यदि विज्ञायते अविद्यमान० · · · न प्राप्नोति ।

अथ विज्ञायते अविद्यमाना . . . न दोषो भवति ।

On P. I, 1, 20—(कथमिदं विज्ञायते . . . . ।)

यदि विज्ञायते दाधाः प्रकृतयः स एव दोषः ।

अथ विज्ञायते दाधां प्रकृतय इति . . . न स्यात् ।

On P. I, 1, 39—(कथमिदं विज्ञायते कृद्यो मान्त इत्याहोस्वित्कृदन्तं यन्मान्तमिति । . . . .)

यदि विज्ञायते कृद्यो मान्त इति . . . . न प्राप्नोति ।

अथ विज्ञायते कृदन्तं यन्मान्तमिति . . . प्राप्नोति ।

On P. I, 1, 50—(सा किं प्रकृतितो भवति . . . आहोस्विदादेशतः . . . ।)

यदि प्रकृतित इको . . . । आदेशतो . . . दोषः ।

On P. I, 1, 52—(किमिदमल्ग्रहणमन्त्यविशेषणमाहोस्विदादेशविशेषणम् । . . .)

यद्यन्त्यविशेषणमादेशो अविशेषितो भवति । . . . .

The difference of expression between the passages quoted from the discussions on P. I, 1, 11 and 65 on the one hand, and from P. I, 1, 39 and 52 on the other, is particularly instructive, because the questions raised and discussed are in either cases exactly the same.

No reader of the Mahâbhâshya can have failed to perceive that frequently objections are raised to Pâṇini's rules, alterations proposed and additional rules suggested. But it not seldom happens that in the course of the discussion these objections are shown to be unfounded, the alterations to be uncalled for, or the additional rules to be unnecessary. And here again we have to notice a striking difference of expression as between the paraphrased sentences and the rest of the Mahâbhâshya; for in the case of the former those objections, &c., are most usually refuted in sentences commencing with the words न वा or सिद्धं तु, generally followed by a noun in the ablative case; while in the latter the same object is attained by such expressions as नैष दोषः, तत्तर्हि वक्तव्यम् । न वक्तव्यम्, followed by a complete sentence which takes the place of the ablative case of the paraphrased sentences. A few examples will suffice to illustrate this difference of expression:—

On P. I, 1, 39 we have the paraphrased sentence न वा संनिपातलक्षणो विधिरनिमित्तं तद्विघातस्येति; on P. I, 1, 20 not paraphrased स तर्हि प्रतिषेधो वक्तव्यः । न वक्तव्यः । घुसंज्ञा कस्मान्न भवति । संनिपातलक्षणो विधिरनिमित्तं तद्विघातस्येत्येवं न भविष्यति.

On P. VI, 4, 130 the paraphrased sentence न वा निर्दिश्यमानस्यादेशत्वात्; on P. I, 1, 47 and 51 not paraphrased नैष दोषः । निर्दिश्यमानस्यादेशा भवन्तीत्येवं न भविष्यति.

On P. VI, 2, 2 the paraphrased sentence सिद्धं तु लक्षणप्रतिपदोक्तयोः प्रतिपदोक्तस्यैव ग्रहणात्; on P. I, 1, 15 not paraphrased न वक्तव्यः । लक्षणप्रतिपदोक्तयोः प्रतिपदोक्तस्येत्येवं न भविष्यति.

On P. VI, 1, 1, the paraphrased sentence सिद्धं तु तद्गुणसंविज्ञानात्पाणिनेर्यथा लोके; on P. I, 1, 27 not paraphrased नैष दोषः । भवति हि बहुव्रीहौ तद्गुणसंविज्ञानमपि.

A common artifice of refuting an objection—less frequently resorted to in the paraphrased sentences than in the rest of the Mahâbhâshya—is to show that that objection has been indirectly guarded against by Pâṇini himself; in other words, to point out a *Jnâpaka*. When this is done in the paraphrased sentences, we find, so far as I have observed, invariably the noun

ज्ञापक followed by another noun in the genetive case; in the remainder of the Mahâbhâshya we always have instead some such verbal phrase as ज्ञापयत्याचार्यः, आचार्यप्रवृत्तिर्ज्ञापयति. Instances of the latter mode of expression are of the most frequent occurrence. From the paraphrased sentences I quote:

On P. I, 1, 11—सप्तम्यामर्थग्रहणं ज्ञापकं प्रत्ययलक्षणप्रतिषेधस्य;

On P. I, 1, 45—विभक्तिविशेषनिर्देशस्तु ज्ञापक उभयसंज्ञात्वस्य;

On P. I, 1, 59—अज्ग्रहणं तु ज्ञापकं रूपस्थानिवद्भावस्य; and ओः पुयण्जिषु वचनं ज्ञापकं णौ स्थानिवद्भावस्य.

And this leads me to draw attention generally to the almost entire absence of verbal forms from the paraphrased sentences, which absence, in my opinion, constitutes one of their chief characteristics of style, as compared with the style of the unparaphrased portion of the Mahâbhâshya. In cases where in the latter we meet with such verbal forms or expressions as प्राप्नोति, विधेयः, नोपपद्यते, वक्तव्यः, इति वक्तव्यम्, न वक्तव्यम्, ग्रहणं न कर्तव्यम्, ग्रहणं शक्यमकर्तुम्, we are sure to meet in the former, nouns such as प्रसङ्गः, विधिः, अनुपपत्तिः, वचनम्, अवचनम्, अग्रहणम्; and in many instances it is altogether left to ourselves to complete the sentence by supplying some verb or phrase such as भवति, भविष्यति, स्यात्, क्रियते, प्राप्नोति, सिध्यति, न सिध्यति, कर्तव्यम्, वक्तव्यम्, इति वक्तव्यम्, &c. On P. I, 1, 8 where the word मुख of Pâṇini's rule is stated to be superfluous, the unparaphrased sentence which contains this statement is मुखग्रहणं शक्यमकर्तुम्; on P. I, 1, 23 where the same remark is made with reference to the words बहु &c. of that rule, the paraphrased sentence made use of for the purpose reads simply बह्वादीनामग्रहणम्. On P. I, 1, 36 and 75 we find the additional or corrective rules अपुरीति वक्तव्यम्, एङ् प्राच्यां देशे शैषिकेष्विति वक्तव्यम्, to which no paraphrase has been attached; so far as my knowledge goes, no paraphrased sentence ever concludes with the phrase इति वक्तव्यम्.

If these considerations should have rendered probable the supposition that the paraphrased sentences are not of Patanjali's authorship, and that the author of the Mahâbhâshya has merely commented on them, and supplemented and corrected the statements contained in them, by his own original remarks, that probability will be raised to a certainty, when we consider the manner in which Patanjali has referred to them and to their author in the uncommented portions of his work. The Mahâbhâshya being a work on Pâṇini's grammar, it is natural that Patanjali, in such words as पठति, करोति, शास्ति, ज्ञापयति, '*he* reads', '*he* teaches,' &c. should have referred to Pâṇini, without being under the necessity of telling us that he was citing or referring to *Pâṇini*. Moreover, I have had occasion to state elsewhere that wherever reference is thus made to Pâṇini, the context would show at once and beyond doubt that the subject of the verbs पठति, करोति &c. can be no other than Pâṇini. But there remain very many verbs of this kind for which it is impossible to supply the subject 'Pâṇini'; in all *these* cases the reference made is, so far as my own observation goes, *invariably* to *paraphrased sentences.* The verbal forms belonging to this class which occur in that part of the Mahâbhâshya which treats of the rules of the first Pâda, are:

On page 55*b* of the Lith. Ben. Ed. पठति; the paraphrased sentence referred to follows immediately upon पठति;

P. 59*b* वक्ष्यति; refers to a paraphrased sentence on the same page;

P. 66*b* वक्ष्यति; to a paraphrased sentence on P. I, 1, 47;
P. 69*a* वक्ष्यति; to a paraphrased sentence on the next page;
P. 72*a* वक्ष्यति; to a paraphrased sentence on P. VI, 1, 101;
P. 77*b* वक्ष्यति; to a paraphrased sentence on P. I. 4, 14;
P. 86*b* वक्ष्यति; to a paraphrased sentence on P. VI. 1, 1;
" वक्ष्यति; to a paraphrased sentence on P. VIII, 3, 59;
P. 88*a* वक्ष्यति; to a paraphrased sentence on P. I, 1, 72;
P. 99*a* वक्ष्यति; to a paraphrased sentence on P. II, 2, 35;
P. 99*b* वक्ष्यति; to a paraphrased sentence on P. II, 2, 35;
" वक्ष्यति; to a paraphrased sentence on P. II, 2, 35;
P. 102*a* वक्ष्यति; to a paraphrased sentence on P. VI, 2, 2;
P. 106*b* वक्ष्यति; to a paraphrased sentence on P. VIII, 2, 3;
P. 117*a* वक्ष्यति; to a paraphrased sentence on P. VI, 4, 72;
P. 133*a* चोदयिष्यति; to a paraphrased sentence on P. I, 1, 56;
P. 139*b* वक्ष्यति; to a paraphrased sentence on P. I, 1, 58;

P. 141*b* वक्ष्यति ; to a paraphrased sentence on P. VIII, 2, 23;
P. 146*b* वक्ष्यति ; to a paraphrased sentence on P. VII, 3, 54;
P. 148*b* वक्ष्यति ; to a paraphrased sentence on P. IV, 3, 163;
P. 156*b* वक्ष्यति ; to a paraphrased sentence on the next page;
P. 157*b* वक्ष्यति ; to a paraphrased sentence on P. VI, 4, 34;
P. 159*b* चोदयिष्यति; to a paraphrased sentence on P. VIII, 2, 107;
P. 164*a* वक्ष्यति ; to a paraphrased sentence on P. VI, 1, 186.

It is hardly necessary to tell the reader that the manner in which Patanjali here invariably speaks of the author of the paraphrased sentences, in no way differs from the manner in which other commentators continually speak, not of themselves, but of those authors on whose works they happen to be commenting, and since there is no doubt that Patanjali *has* commented on those sentences, it is natural to conclude that those sentences are not his own, but are the work of *another*. And this conclusion is further strengthened, when we find that in such expressions as पठिष्यति ह्याचार्यः *e.g.* on page 75 *b* of the Benares Edn., or वक्ष्यति ह्याचार्यः : *e.g.* on pages 143*b* and 151*a*, the author of those sentences* is actually spoken of by Patanjali as the Âchârya, in the same way in which Patanjali elsewhere speaks of the Âchârya Pâṇini.

The first part of our enquiry is drawing to a close. Considering it unlikely that an author in the composition of one and the same work should have adopted two methods of discussion so different as those which Patanjali would seem to have adopted in his Mahâbhâshya, we ventured to assume that those portions of the Mahâbhâshya which have been furnished by him with paraphrase and comment, were not his own. That assumption we tried to render probable by pointing out that the manner in which Patanjali in various passages of his work has been paraphrasing and commenting, admits of a reasonable explanation only when we assume that he was commenting on and paraphrasing the words of another. We then showed that the paraphrased portions of the Mahâbhâshya in style and language differ from the rest of that work as we

* See on P. VI, 1, 129; VI, 4, 104; and VI, 1, 12.

might expect the works of two different authors to differ from each other. And we finally pointed out that by the manner in which he continually refers to and quotes the paraphrased sentences and their author, Patanjali himself has clearly shown to us that that author must be another than himself. Fortunately we are not left without the means of ascertaining who that author was. For since Patanjali, when *e.g.* quoting on P. I, 1, 34, a paraphrased sentence from the discussion on P. VIII, 3, 13, incidentally, but obliged to be more explicit than usual because only in the preceding line and for one and the same purpose he had been quoting the Âchârya Pâṇini, has told us that that paraphrased sentence is the Vârttikakâra's, it is clear that that author was called *Vârttikakâra*. And since the same Patanjali, after having on P. III, 2, 118, in his usual manner paraphrased a sentence, has in the sequel informed us that that sentence is Kâtyâyana's, it is equally clear that the name of that Vârttikakâra was *Kâtyâyana*.

The conclusion then at which we have arrived is this, that the paraphrased sentences which we meet with in the Mahâbhâshya belong to Kâtyâyana, the author of the Vârttikas; and this conclusion furnishes us with a means, in my opinion the *only* means, of reconstructing from the text of the Mahâbhâshya, as it has been handed down to us in MS., the text of the Vârttikas of Kâtyâyana. We may as yet consider it matter for further enquiry whether *all* the Vârttikas of Kâtyâyana have been recorded by Patanjali; but wherever in the Mahâbhâshya we meet with a paraphrased statement, of which Patanjali does not tell us explicitly that it belongs to another or to others, or of which the context does not prove clearly and beyond doubt that it is a quotation from the work of another, we shall regard ourselves as bound to assume that such statement is Kâtyâyana's, or in other words, that it is a Vârttika or part of one. On the other hand, we shall not allow ourselves to regard as a Vârttika of Kâtyâyana any statement unless it be accompanied by a paraphrase.* In

* If in accordance with this principle we examine the passages from the Mahâbhâshya quoted by Prof. Goldstücker in notes 141—152 of

applying this principle, we may occasionally find it difficult to decide whether a particular statement should be regarded as merely paraphrasing another statement by which it is preceded, or as an explanatory remark such as an author might think it necessary to append to a statement previously made by himself. But, on the one hand, to judge from my own experience, such cases are exceedingly rare; on the other hand, the more we become familiar with the manner, the style, and the language of Kâtyâyana by the study of what undoubtedly is his, the easier and the more ready will be our decision in cases which at first sight may appear to us doubtful.

There is yet another difficulty which is intimately connected with and which results from the manner in which Patanjali has paraphrased the Vârttikas of Kâtyâyana. I have found it convenient to employ throughout the preceding investigation the word *paraphrase,* but it would have been more correct to say that frequently Patanjali does not paraphrase but literally repeats the words of the Vârttika which he happens to make use of. If I might venture to give a reason for his doing so, I would say that Patanjali adopted that practice in order to apprise us of the fact that he was giving us not his own arguments but those of Kâtyâyana; in other words, to save the literary property of that scholar. However this may be, there can be no doubt that the very practice which he adopted, through the carelessness of the copyists, has in many cases led to the disappearance of Vârttikas from our MSS., and consequently from the only complete edition of the Mahâbhâshya which has been published up to the present. One example will suffice to prove this.

---

his Pâṇini, we find that Prof. Goldstücker has correctly termed Vârttikas इन्धेश्छन्दो° on P. I, 2, 6 (note 141); इतराच्छन्दसि° on P. VII, 1, 26 (note 142); यरोऽनुनासिके° on P. VIII, 4, 45, (note 143); वा गोमयेषु on P. IV, 2, 129 (note 152). On the other hand, the statements विकिरो वेति वक्तव्यम् on P. VI, 1, 150 (note 145); आश्चर्यमद्भुत इति व° on P. VI, 1, 147 (note 147); भोज्यमभ्यवहार्यमिति व° on P. VII, 3, 69 (note 148); पथ्यध्याय° इति व° on P. IV, 2, 129 (note 152); which also have been termed Vârttikas by Prof. Goldstücker and other scholars, are no Vârttikas, but are Patanjali's.

On pages 149 *a* and *b* of the Lithog. Benares Edn., we read as follows:—

किं प्रयोजनम् । क्सलोपः सलोपे । क्सलोपः सलोपे प्रयोजनम् । . . . . दध आकारलोप आदिचतुर्थत्वे प्रयोजनम् । . . . . . हलो यमां यमि लोपे प्रयोजनम् । . . . . अल्लोपणिलोपौ संयोगान्तलोपप्रभृतिषु प्रयोजनम् । . . . . द्विर्वचनादीनि च प्रयोजनानि न पठितव्यानि भवन्ति . . . . । वरेयलोपस्वरवर्जम् । वरेयलोपं स्वरं च वर्जयित्वा ।

According to what I have said in the preceding, this passage would seem to contain only *two* Vârttikas, *viz.* क्सलोपः सलोपे and वरेयलोपस्वरवर्जम्, for apparently only these two statements have been paraphrased by Patanjali. A comparison of other Vârttikas of Kâtyâyana (on P. I, 1, 21, 39, &c.) would make us feel inclined to read the first of these Vârttikas प्रयोजनं क्सलोपः सलोपे, and we would willingly recognize Vârttikas also in दध आकारलोप°, हलो यमां°, अल्लोप°, and द्विर्वचनादीनि°, were we not forbidden to do so by the result of our enquiry. We now turn to Prof. Goldstücker's photo-lithograph copy of the Mahâbhâshya, and find that there the same passage is read thus:—

किं प्रयोजनम् । प्रयोजनं क्सलोपः सलोपे । क्सलोपः सलोपे प्रयोजनम् । . . . . . दध आकारलोप आदिचतुर्थत्वे प्रयोजनम् । . . . . . हलो यमां यमि लोपे २ प्रयोजनम् । . . . अल्लोपणिलोपौ संयोगान्तलोपप्रभृतिषु २ प्रयोजनम् । . . . द्विर्वचनादीनि च । द्विर्वचनादीनि च न पठितव्यानि भवन्ति । . . . . . वरेयलोपस्वरवर्जम् । वरेयलोपं स्वरं च वर्जयित्वा ॥

Here we find that the first Vârttika is really read as we expected that it should be read, प्रयोजनं क्सलोपः सलोपे, and we perceive at once that the first word प्रयोजनं has been omitted in the Benares edition because it was preceded by the same word प्रयोजनं in किं प्रयोजनम्. We further see from the figure २ after लोपे and प्रभृतिषु that the words हलो यमां यमि लोपे and अल्लोपणिलोपौ संयोगान्तलोपप्रभृतिषु have to be read twice; and the words

द्विर्वचनादीनि च we find actually written twice. Such being the case, the result of our enquiry tells us that हलो यमां यमि लोपे, अलोपणिलोपौ संयोगान्तलोपप्रभृतिषु, and द्विर्वचनादीनि च which we were inclined to regard as Vârttikas, *are* Vârttikas, omitted in the Benares edition, or in the MSS. from which it has been prepared, because the paraphrases by which those Vârttikas are followed commence with identically the same words. And having found it proved in this manner, that at least three of the four statements which we were inclined to regard as Vârttikas, *are* Vârttikas, we shall not I trust be accused of rashness when we venture to assume that also the fourth of those statements, दध आकारलोप आदिचतुर्थत्वे, is really a Vârttika, omitted also in the photo-lithograph copy, because the writer forgot to write the figure २ after the word आदिचतुर्थत्वे. The Vârttikas which the above passage contains, are therefore not two, but six:

1. प्रयोजनं क्सलोपः सलोपे.
2. दध आकारलोप आदिचतुर्थत्वे.
3. हलो यमां यमि लोपे.
4. अलोपणिलोपौ संयोगान्तलोपप्रभृतिषु.
5. द्विर्वचनादीनि च.
6. वरेयलोपस्वरवर्जम्.

In a similar manner Vârttikas have disappeared on page 162*a* of the Benares edition, on page 168*b*, 169*b*, 173*b*, 177*b*, and elsewhere. Here then our only safeguard is not to trust to one or two indifferent MSS., but to compare in every instance the best and oldest MSS. which we may be able to lay hold of.

III.

There is in my opinion no better way of testing the soundness of the conclusion at which we have arrived in the preceding, than practically to apply the principle with which it has furnished us, for the reconstruction of Kâtyâyana's Vârttikas. But as want of space would forbid such a reconstruction on any large scale, I am obliged to confine my attempt in this direction to a small portion of the Mahâbhâshya. I shall choose for the purpose first the 7th Âhnika of the first Pâda, which treats of Pâṇini's rules I, 1, 45—55. After having pointed out the Vârttikas which occur in the discussion of each rule, I shall, in as few words as possible, point out their tendency, and shall show (in italics) what Patanjali's views are in regard to them, or whether he has raised any points of discussion regarding the rules of Pâṇini, which have not been noticed by Kâtyâyana; but I shall not think it necessary expressly to state in each case that Patanjali has simply commented on or adopted a particular Vârttika. In notes I shall indicate whether any portions of the discussion have incidentally been called Vârttikas by Kaiyaṭa, Nâgojîbhaṭṭa or Bhaṭṭojidîkshita (in his Śabdakaustubha), and shall also state what Vârttikas or other remarks from the Mahâbhâshya the editors of the Calcutta edition of Pâṇini have thought fit to append to their gloss. Having, in this manner, gone through the whole of the 7th Âhnika, I shall subject the discussions on some other rules of the first Pâda to a similar examination.

P. I, 1, 45—इग्यणः संप्रसारणम् ||

Vârttikas:

(*a*) संप्रसारणसंज्ञायां वाक्यस्य संज्ञा चेद्वर्णविधिः ||

(*b*) वर्णसंज्ञा चेन्निर्वृत्तिः ||

(*c*) विभक्तिविशेषनिर्देशस्तु ज्ञापक उभयसंज्ञात्वस्य ||

(*a*) and (*b*) state the objections to which the two possible interpretations of Pâṇini's rule would be liable; (*c*) shows why both interpretations are nevertheless admissible.

Patanjali agrees with Kâtyâyana; and shows subsequently how the objections to either interpretation may be refuted also in other ways.

Note.—The Calcutta edition gives no Vârttikas, nor any remarks of Patanjali's.

P. I, 1, 46— आद्यन्तौ टकितौ ॥

Vârttikas :

(*a*) टकितोराद्यन्तविधाने प्रत्ययप्रतिषेधः ॥

(*b*) परवचनात्सिद्धमिति चेन्नापवादत्वात् ॥

(*c*) सिद्धं तु षष्ठ्यधिकारे वचनात् ॥

(*d*) आद्यन्तयोर्वा षष्ठ्यर्थत्वात्तदभावेऽसंप्रत्ययः ॥

Patanjali commences with remarks on the terms of Pâṇini's rule and on Âgamas in general.

(*a*) suggests a correction, and (*b*) obviates an objection that might be raised to (*a*).

(*c*) and (*d*) show in different ways that the correction suggested in *(a)* is unnecessary.

Note.—The Calcutta edition gives the Vârttikas (*a*) and (*c*), but states in the words इति भाष्यम् that (*c*) is a remark of Patanjali's.

P. I, 1, 47— मिदचोऽन्त्यात्परः ॥

Vârttikas :

(*a*) मिदचोऽन्त्यात्परः स्थानपरप्रत्ययस्यापवादः ॥

(*b*) अन्त्यात्पूर्वो मस्जेर्मिदनुषङ्गसंयोगादिलोपार्थम् ॥

(*c*) भर्जिमर्च्योश्च ॥

(*d*) अभक्ते दीर्घनलोपस्वरणत्वानुस्वारशीभावाः ॥

(*e*) परादौ गुणवृद्ध्यौत्त्वदीर्घनलोपानुस्वारशीभावेनकारप्रतिषेधाः ॥

(*f*) पूर्वान्ते नपुंसकोपसर्जनह्रस्वत्वं द्विगुस्वरश्च ॥

(*g*) न वा बहिरङ्गलक्षणत्वात् ॥

(*a*) states the object of Pâṇini's rule.

(*b*) and (*c*) correct that rule.*

Patanjali refutes (c).

---

* The Vârttika (*c*) presupposes another etymology of मर्चि than the one given in Uṇâdisûtra IV. 70.

(*d*—*f*) consider the question whether the augment (नुम्) is to stand by itself or to be attached to what follows or precedes it; the question is decided in favour of the last alternative, for the faults arising on that alternative are refuted in (*g*).

Patanjali agrees with Kâtyâyana and supports the conclusion at which he has arrived by an argument of his own.

Note.—(*b*) is quoted by Patanjali on P. I, 1, 7 (वक्ष्यत्येतत् । अन्त्यात्पूर्वो॰ र्थमिति) ; (*b*) is called a Vârttika by Bhaṭṭojidîkshita; (*d*) and (*e*) by Nâgojîbhaṭṭa. The Calcutta edition gives only the Vârttikas (*b*) and (*c*), the former incorrectly. The Nyâya which it quotes is identical in purpose with remarks made by Patanjali.

P. I, 1, 48—एच इग्घ्रस्वादेशे ||

Vârttikas:

(*a*) एच इग्वचनं सवर्णाकारनिवृत्त्यर्थम् ||

(*b*) दीर्घाप्रसङ्गस्तु निवर्तकत्वात् ||

(*c*) सिद्धमेङः सस्थानत्वात् ||

(*d*) ऐचोश्चोत्तरभूयस्त्वात् ||*

(*a*) states the objects of Pàṇini's rule.

(*b*) refutes a possible objection.

(*c*) and (*d*) show that the objects for which the rule has been given are attained without it, and that the rule is therefore unnecessary.

Note.—(*c*) and (*d*) are quoted on Śivasûtra 3 and 4. The Calcutta edition gives no Vârttikas, nor any remarks of Patanjali's.

---

* The short substitute for ऐ is इ, because इ forms a larger portion of ऐ than अ. The word अवरतः of Patanjali's gloss can in my opinion only mean 'less in number.' One calls a village a Brâhmin-village, although some of its inhabitants belong to other castes, because the number of Brâhmins who live in it, is greater than the number of inhabitants belonging to other castes. For a different interpretation, see *Ind. Stud.* XIII, p. 333, note.

P. I, 1, 49—षष्ठी स्थानेयोगा ||

Vârttikas:

(*a*) षष्ठीस्थानेयोगवचनं नियमार्थम् ||

(*b*) अवयवषष्ठ्यादिष्वतिप्रसङ्गः शासो गोह इति ||

(*c*) अवयवषष्ठ्यादीनां चाप्राप्तिर्योगस्यासंदिग्धत्वात् ||

(*d*) विशिष्टा वा षष्ठी स्थानेयोगा ||

Patanjali annotates on the term स्थानेयोगा.

(*a*) states the object of Pâṇini's rule.

(*b*) suggests the objection that if the object of the rule be correctly stated in (*a*), the rule is too widely applicable.

(*c*) refutes that objection.

Patanjali supports (*c*) *by additional arguments.*

(*d*) suggests a different way of obviating the objection raised in (*b*).

Patanjali shows that the rule, in the sense ascribed to it, is superfluous, and will retain it only because its adoption allows us to dispense with the Paribhâshâ निर्दिश्यमानस्यादेशा भवन्ति, *with which Paribhâshâ he considers it to be identical in meaning.*

Note.—(c) and *(d)* are called Vârttikas by Nâgojîbhaṭṭa.—The Calcutta Edn. gives only the Paribhâshâ निर्दिश्यमानस्यादेशा भवन्ति.

P. I, 1, 50—स्थानेऽन्तरतमः ||

Vârttikas:

(*a*) स्थानिन एकत्वनिर्देशादनेकादेशनिर्देशाच्च सर्वप्रसङ्गस्तस्मात्स्थानेऽन्तरतमवचनं नियमार्थम् ||

(*b*) स्थानेऽन्तरतमनिर्वर्तके सर्वस्थानिनिवृत्तिः ||

(*c*) निर्वृत्तप्रतिपत्तौ निर्वृत्तिः ||

(*d*) अनर्थकं च ||

(*e*) उक्तं वा ||

(*f*) प्रत्यात्मवचनं च ||

(*g*) प्रत्यात्मवचनमशिष्यं स्वभावसिद्धत्वात् ॥

(*h*) अन्तरतमवचनं च ॥

(*i*) व्यञ्जनस्वरव्यतिक्रमे च तत्कालप्रसङ्गः ॥

(*k*) अक्षु चानेकवर्णादेशेषु ॥

(*l*) गुणवृद्ध्येज्भावेषु च ॥

(*m*) ऋवर्णस्य गुणवृद्धिप्रसङ्गे सर्वप्रसङ्गो ऽविशेषात् ॥

(*n*) न वा ऋवर्णस्य स्थाने रपरप्रसङ्गादवर्णस्यान्तर्यम् ॥

(*o*) सर्वादेशप्रसङ्गस्त्वनेकाल्त्वात् ॥

(*p*) न चानेकाल्त्वस्य तदाश्रयत्वादृवर्णादेशस्याविघातः ॥

(*q*) संप्रयोगो वा नष्टाश्वदग्धरथवत् ॥

(*r*) एजवर्णयोरादेशे ऽवर्णं स्थानिनो ऽवर्णप्रधानत्वात् ॥

(*s*) सिद्धं तूभयान्तर्यात् ॥

Patanjali gives an example for Pâṇini's rule which does not result from any other rule, and which therefore proves that the rule is necessary; he shows why स्थाने, *which we read in the preceding rule, has been repeated here; and why Pâṇini has employed the superlative* अन्तरतम.

(*a*) shows why Pâṇini was obliged to give this rule, and states the object of the rule.

Patanjali, having accepted this, discusses the question whether the rule should be read स्थानेऽन्तरतमे *or* स्थानेऽन्तरतमः, *both readings being possible when the rules of Sandhi as between this and the following rule are observed.*

(*b—d*). Does this rule teach something independently of other rules, or does it give certain directions regarding substitutes that have been taught in other rules? The question is decided in favour of the latter alternative, for the objections which were raised to that alternative, are in (*e*) met by a reference to a statement made before (Vârt. (*r*) on P. I, 1, 3).

Patanjali, when commenting on (*b*), *brings forward another objection in addition to the one raised in the Vârttika.*

(*f*) suggests a correction of Pâṇini's rule, which correction (*g*) shows to be unnecessary.

(*h*) states that Pâṇini's rule is unnecessary, because what is taught in it results from the ordinary practice of life. If the rule be nevertheless adopted, it is liable to the objections stated in (*i*), (*k*), and (*l*).

Patanjali refutes these three objections.

(*m*) suggests the desirability of making a rule that should teach what the Guṇa and Vṛiddhi of ऋ are; (*n*) and (*q*) show that no such rule is required.

Patanjali shows, by giving an additional reason, that such a rule is not required.

(*o*) states an objection which the adoption of (*n*) would give rise to; (*p*) refutes that objection.

(*r*) raises an objection to Pâṇini's rule, regarding the substitute for एच् + अ; (*s*) refutes that objection.

Note.—(*l*) is called a Vârttika by Nâgojibhaṭṭa; (*o*), (*p*), and (*q*) are called Vârttikas by Bhaṭṭojidîkshita. The Calcutta Edn. gives no Vârttikas; the Paribhâshâ quoted is taken from Patanjali's remarks.

P. I, 1, 51—उरण्रपरः ||

Vârttikas:

(*a*) उरण्रपरवचनमन्यनिवृत्त्यर्थमिति चेदुदात्तादिषु दोषः ||

(*b*) य उः स्थानेऽण् स रपर इति चेद्गुणवृद्ध्योरवर्णाप्रतिपत्तिः ||

(*c*) सिद्धं तु प्रसङ्गे रपरत्वात् ||

(*d*) आदेशो रपर इति चेदीरिविधिषु रपरप्रतिषेधः ||

(*e*) उदात्तादिषु च ||

(*f*) एकादेशस्योपसंख्यानम् ||

(*g*) अवयवग्रहणात्सिद्धमिति चेदादेशे रान्तप्रतिषेधः ||

(*h*) अभक्ते दीर्घलत्वयगभ्यस्तस्वरहलादिःशेषविसर्जनीयप्रतिषेधः प्रत्ययाव्यवस्था च ||

(*i*) पूर्वान्ते चैवधारणं विसर्जनीयप्रतिषेधो यक्स्वरश्च ॥

(*k*) परादावकारलोपीत्वपुक्प्रतिषेधश्चङ्चुपधाह्रस्वत्वमिटोऽव्यव-
स्थाभ्यासलोपोऽभ्यस्ततादिस्वरो दीर्घत्वं च ॥

(*a*) and (*b*) state the objections to which two possible interpretations of Pâṇini's rule would be liable; (*c*) suggests the correct interpretation of that rule.

(*d*) and (*e*) refute the possible objection that Pâṇini should have said merely ऋ रपरः (*i. e.* उरादेशो रपरः) instead of उरण्रपरः. (*f*) demands an additional rule, and (*g*) obviates an objection to that rule.

*Patanjali shows that the additional rule is not required.** (*h—k*) discuss the same question in regard to the augment इ, which had been discussed in Vârttikas (*d—f*) on I, 1, 47, with regard to the augment नुम्, without distinctly deciding which alternative should be adopted.

Patanjali refutes some of the objections raised to the first and last alternatives, and all those to which the adoption of the view expressed in (i) was stated to be liable.

Note.—(*b*) is called a Vârttika by Bhaṭṭojidîkshita, and (*d*), (*h*), and (*k*) are called Vârttikas by Nâgojîbhaṭṭa. The Calcutta Edn. gives the four Vârttikas (*d—g*), the last of them incorrectly.

P. I, 1, 52—अलोऽन्त्यस्य ॥

Vârttikas:

(*a*) अलोऽन्त्यस्येति स्थाने विज्ञातस्यानुसंहारः ॥

(*b*) इतरथा ह्यनिष्टप्रसङ्गः ॥

(*c*) योगशेषे च ॥

Patanjali discusses the question whether अलः *is a genitive qualifying* अन्त्यस्य, *or a nominative (plural) qualifying the Âdeśa.*

---

* Patanjali in his remarks quotes a Vârttika on P. VIII, 4, 31 which he paraphrases in the usual manner.

(*a—c*) show the correct way of applying Pâṇini's rule.

Note.—The Calcutta Edn. gives no Vârttikas.

P. I, 1, 53—ङिच्च ||

Vârttika :

(*a*) तातङि ङित्करणस्य सावकाशत्वाद्विप्रतिषेधात्सर्वादेशः ||

(*a*) shows why तातङ् is not substituted for the final only, in other words, refutes an objection that might be raised to Pâṇini's rule.

Patanjali rejects Kâtyâyana's explanation, and substitutes for it another.

Note.—The Vârttika is given inaccurately in the Calcutta Edn.

P. I, 1, 54—आदेः परस्य ||

Vârttika :

(*a*) अलोऽन्त्यस्यादेः परस्यानेकाल्शित्सर्वस्येत्यपवादविप्रतिषेधात्सर्वादेशः ||

(*a*) a remark regarding the scope of this rule and of the next.

Note.—The Calcutta Edn. does not give the Vârttika.

P. I, 1, 55—अनेकाल्शित्सर्वस्य ||

No Vârttika.

Patanjali shows that शित्, *since it would otherwise be superfluous, indicates the existence of the Paribhâshâ* नानुबन्धकृतमनेकाल्त्वं भवति, *and he states that that Paribhâshâ renders two Vârttikas (on III, 1, 94 and I, 1, 20) unnecessary.*

Note.—The Calcutta Edn. gives the Paribhâshâ.

The above are all the rules discussed in the 7th Âhnika; in the following I propose to examine the discussions on P. I, 1, 1; 6; 25; 36; 39; 65; 68; 72; and 75.

P. I, 1, 1—वृद्धिरादैच् ||

Vârttikas :

(*a*) संज्ञाधिकारः संज्ञासंप्रत्ययार्थः ||

(*b*) इतरथा ह्यसंप्रत्ययो यथा लोके ||

(c) संज्ञासंज्ञ्यसंदेहश्च ||

(d) आचार्याचारात्संज्ञासिद्धिः ||

(e) यथा लौकिकवैदिकेषु ||

(f) संज्ञासंज्ञ्यसंदेहश्च ||

(g) अनाकृतिः ||

(h) लिङ्गेन वा ||

(i) सतो वृद्ध्यादिषु संज्ञाभावात्तदाश्रय इतरेतराश्रयत्वादप्रसिद्धिः ||

(k) सिद्धं तु नित्यशब्दत्वात् ||

(l) किमर्थं शास्त्रमिति चेन्निवर्तकत्वात्सिद्धम् ||

(m) अन्यत्र सहवचनात्समुदाये संज्ञाप्रसङ्गः ||

(n) प्रत्यवयवं च वाक्यपरिसमाप्तेः ||

(o) आकारस्य तपरकरणं सवर्णार्थम् ||

Patanjali justifies the च् *of* आदैच्; *he discusses the question whether* आदैच् *means every* आ, ऐ, *and* औ, *or only those which are taught in grammar by the term* वृद्धि.

(a) and (b) demand a Saṃjnâdhikâra, and (c) demands besides that it should be stated distinctly what is meant to be the Saṃjnâ, whether वृद्धि or आदैच्. (d—h) refute (a—c).

Patanjali does not approve of the way in which Kâtyâyana has refuted (a—c), and he therefore refutes those Vârttikas differently.

(i) raises an objection, which is refuted in (k); (l) answers a question to which (k) gives rise.

(m) and (n) refute the possible objection that Pâṇini should have said प्रत्येकम् in this and the next rule.

Patanjali does not approve of the way in which Kâtyâyana has refuted the objection.

(o) states why Pâṇini has affixed त् to आ.

Patanjali does not approve of the Vârttika, and gives another reason for the त्.

Note.—(*a*) and (*b*) are called Vârttikas by Kaiyaṭa; (*i*), (*k*), (*l*), and (*o*) by Bhaṭṭojidîkshita. The Calcutta Edn. gives the Vârttikas (*a*), (*c*), and (*o*), the last incorrectly; it also gives as a Vârttika प्रत्येकं गुणवृद्धिसंज्ञे भवतः, but this is a remark of Patanjali's by which he introduces the Vârttika (*m*).

P. I, 1, 6—दीधीवेवीटाम् ||

Vârttikas :

(*a*) दिधीवेव्योश्छन्दोविषयत्वाद्दृष्टानुविधित्वाच्च छन्दसो ऽदीधेदवीधयुरिति गुणदर्शनादप्रतिषेधः ||

(*b*) दीध्यदिति च श्यन्व्यत्ययेन ||

(*a*) and (*b*) show that दीधीवेवी may be omitted from Pâṇini's rule.

Patanjali states that इट् is likewise unnecessary.

Note.—The Calcutta Edn. quotes part of (*a*) but states that it is a remark of Patanjali's.

P. I, 1, 25—डति च ||

No Vârttika.

Patanjali shows that either the डति of I, 1, 23 or the डति of this rule may be omitted.

Note.—The Calcutta Edn. ascribes the remark इदं ङतिग्रहणं &c., correctly to Patanjali.

P. I, 1, 36—अन्तरं बहिर्योगोपसंव्यानयोः ||

Vârttikas :

(*a*) उपसंव्यानग्रहणमनर्थकं बहिर्योगेण कृतत्वात् ||

(*b*) न वा शाटकयुगाद्यर्थम् ||

(*c*) वाप्रकरणे तीयस्य ङित्सूपसंख्यानम् ||

(*a*) suggests a correction of Pâṇini's rule, which correction (*b*) shows to be unnecessary.

Patanjali adopts the correction proposed in (a) and rejects therefore the word उपसंव्यान from Pâṇini's rule.

Patanjali gives the additional rule अपुरीति वक्तव्यम्.

(*c*) suggests an additional rule.

Note.—(*b*) is called Vârttika by Kaiyaṭa and Bhaṭṭojidîkshita. Bhaṭṭojidîkshita also calls अपुरीति वक्तव्यम् a Vârttika; it is given as a Vârttika also in the Calcutta Edn., but the Calcutta Edn. is wrong when it says that it has been called a Vârttika by Kaiyaṭa. (*c*) is given as a Vârttika in the Calcutta Edn., but inaccurately.

P. I, 1, 39—कृन्मेजन्तः ॥

Vârttikas:

(*a*) कृन्मेजन्तश्चानिकारोकारप्रकृतिः ॥

(*b*) अनन्यप्रकृतिरिति वा ॥

(*c*) न वा संनिपातलक्षणो विधिरनिमित्तं तद्विघातस्येति ॥

(*d*) प्रयोजनं ह्रस्वत्वं तुग्विधेर्ग्रामणिकुलम् ॥

(*e*) नलोपो वृत्रहभिः ॥

(*f*) उदुपधत्वमकित्त्वस्य निकुचिते ॥

(*g*) नाभावो यञि दीर्घत्वस्यामुना ॥

(*h*) आत्त्वं कित्त्वस्योपादास्त ॥

(*i*) तिसृचतसृत्वं ङीब्विधेः ॥

(*k*) तस्य दोषो वर्णाश्रयः प्रत्ययो वर्णविघातस्य ॥

(*l*) आत्त्वं पुग्विधेः क्रापयति ॥

(*m*) पुग्घ्रस्वत्वस्यादीदपत् ॥

(*n*) स्यदाद्यकारष्टाब्विधेः ॥

(*o*) इड्विधिराकारलोपस्य ययिवान् ॥

(*p*) मतुब्विभक्त्युदात्तत्वं पूर्वनिघातस्य ॥

(*q*) नदीह्रस्वत्वं संबुद्धिलोपस्य ॥

Patanjali states the objections to which the two possible

interpretations of Pâṇini's rule would be liable and shows that both interpretations nevertheless are admissible.

(*a*) suggests a correction of Pâṇini's rule, which correction is improved on in (*b*); (*c*) states that the corrections suggested in (*a*) and (*b*) are unnecessary as soon as the Saṃnipâta-paribhâshâ is adopted; (*d—i*) give examples for that Paribhâshâ, and (*k—q*) enumerate exceptional cases in which the Paribhâshâ must not be applied.

Patanjali shows that the examples for the Paribhâshâ which have been given by Kâtyâyana can be formed without that Paribhâshâ, but shows by giving three different examples that the Paribhâshâ must be adopted nevertheless.

Note.—(*d*) and (*k*) are called Vârttikas by Nâgojîbhaṭṭa in his Paribhâshenduśekhara. The Calcutta Edn. gives (*a*) and (*b*), and the Paribhâshâ contained in (*c*).

P. I, 1, 65—अलोऽन्त्यात्पूर्व उपधा ||

Vârttikas :

(*a*) उपधासंज्ञायामल्ग्रहणमन्त्यनिर्देशश्चेत्संघातप्रतिषेधः ||

(*b*) अन्त्यविज्ञानात्सिद्धमिति चेन्नानर्थकेऽलोऽन्त्यविधिरनभ्यासविकारे ||

(*c*) प्रयोजनमव्यक्तानुकरणस्यात इतौ ||

(*d*) ध्वसोरेद्धावभ्यासलोपश्च ||

(*e*) आपि लोपोऽकोऽनचि ||

(*f*) अत्र लोपोऽभ्यासस्य ||*

(*g*) अलोऽन्त्यात्पूर्वोऽलुपधेति वा ||

(*h*) अवचनाल्लोकविज्ञानात्सिद्धम् ||

It might appear as if Pâṇini's rule should either be restricted (*a*); or altered (*g*). In reality it is quite correct (*h*). (*b*) shows, by quoting a Paribhâshâ, how (*a*) cannot be refuted; and (*c—f*) give examples for the Paribhâshâ cited in (*b*).

* MS. of I. O. reads अत्र लोपोऽभ्यासस्य । अत्र लोपोऽभ्यासस्येत्य°.

Patanjali objects to all the examples given in (c—f) and rejects therefore the Paribhâshâ cited in (b).

Note.—(*g*) is called Vârttika by Nâgojibhaṭṭa.—The Calcutta Edn. gives (*a*), and the Paribhâshâ contained in (*b*).

P. I, 1, 68—स्वं रूपं शब्दस्याशब्दसंज्ञा ||

Vârttikas:

(*a*) शब्देनार्थगतेरर्थे कार्यस्यासंभवात्तद्वाचिनः संज्ञाप्रतिषेधार्थं स्वरूपवचनम् ||

(*b*) न वा शब्दपूर्वको ह्यर्थे संप्रत्ययस्तस्मादर्थनिवृत्तिः ||

(*c*) शब्दसंज्ञाप्रतिषेधानर्थक्यं वचनप्रामाण्यात् ||

(*d*) मन्त्राद्यर्थमिति चेच्छास्त्रसामर्थ्यादर्थगतेः सिद्धम् ||

(*e*) सित्तद्विशेषाणां वृक्षाद्यर्थम् ||

(*f*) पित्पर्यायवचनस्य च स्वाद्यर्थम् ||

(*g*) जित्पर्यायवचनस्यैव राजाद्यर्थम् ||

(*h*) झित्तस्य च तद्विशेषाणां च मत्स्याद्यर्थम् ||

Patanjali shows that रूपम् *conveys the sense conveyed by the Paribhâshâ* अर्थवद्ग्रहणे नानर्थकस्य, *and renders that Paribhâshâ unnecessary.*

(*a*) shows why it was necessary for Pâṇini to give this rule;
(*b—d*) show that the rule can be dispensed with.
(*e—h*) give additional rules.

Patanjali corrects the additional rule (*h*) *by adding to it.*

Note.—The Calcutta Edn. gives the Vârttikas (*e—h*), and (inaccurately) Patanjali's remark on (*h*). It also cites the Paribhâshâ mentioned by Patanjali.

P. I, 1, 72—येन विधिस्तदन्तस्य ||

Vârttikas:

(*a*) येन विधिस्तदन्तस्येति चेद्ग्रहणोपाधीनां तदन्तोपाधिप्रसङ्गः ||

(*b*) सिद्धं तु विशेषणविशेष्ययोर्यथेष्टत्वात् ॥

(*c*) समासप्रत्ययविधौ प्रतिषेधः ॥

(*d*) उगिद्वर्णग्रहणवर्जम् ॥

(*e*) अकच्प्रभृतः सर्वनामाव्ययधातुविधावुपसंख्यानम् ॥

(*f*) सिद्धं तु तदन्तान्तवचनात् ॥

(*g*) तदेकदेशविज्ञानाद्वा सिद्धम् ॥

(*h*) प्रयोजनं सर्वनामाव्ययसंज्ञायाम् ॥*

(*i*) उपपदविधौ भयाढ्यादिग्रहणम् ॥†

(*k*) ङीब्विधावुगिद्ग्रहणम् ॥‡

(*l*) प्रतिषेधे स्वस्रादिग्रहणम् ॥‡

(*m*) अपरिमाणबिस्तादिग्रहणं च प्रतिषेधे ॥§

(*n*) दितिः ॥‖

(*o*) रोण्या अण् ॥

(*p*) तस्य च ॥

(*q*) रथसीताहलेभ्यो यद्विधौ ॥¶

(*r*) सुसर्वार्धदिक्शब्देभ्यो जनपदस्य ॥**

(*s*) ऋतोर्वृद्धिमद्विधाववयवानाम् ॥††

(*t*) ठञ्विधौ संख्यायाः ॥‡‡

(*u*) धर्मान्नञः ॥§§

---

* MS. of I. O. प्रयोजनं सर्वनामाव्ययसंज्ञायां सर्वनामाव्ययसंज्ञायां प्रयोजनं.

† MS. of I. O. उपपदविधौ भयाढ्यादिग्रहणं २ प्रयोजनम्.

‡ Should be read twice both in the Benares edition and in the I. O. MS.

§ MS. of I. O. अपरिमाणबिस्तादिग्रहणं च प्रतिषेधे २ प्रयोजनम् ॥

‖ MS of I. O. दिति दितिग्रहणं च प्रयोजनम्. Bhattojid. reads दितिः.

¶ MS. of I. O. रथसीताहलेभ्यो यद्विधौ २ प्रयोजनम्.

** MS. of I. O. सुसर्वार्द्धदिक्शब्देभ्यो जनपदस्य २ प्रयोजनम्.

†† MS. of I. O. ऋतोर्वृद्धिमद्विधाववयवानां २ प्रयोजनम्.

‡‡ MS. of I. O. ठञ्विधौ संख्यायाः २ प्रयोजनम्.

§§ MS. of I. O. धर्मान्नञः २ प्रयोजनम्.

(v) पदाङ्गाधिकारे तस्य च तदुत्तरपदस्य च ॥

(w) प्रयोजनमिष्टकेषीकामालानां चिततूलभारिषु ॥*

(x) प्रयोजनं महदप्स्वसृनप्तृणां दीर्घविधौ ॥†

(y) पद्युष्मदस्मदस्थ्याद्यनडुहो नुम् ॥‡

(z) सुपथिमथिपुंगोसखिचतुरनडुत्त्रिग्रहणम् ॥§

(aa) त्यदादिविधिभसादिस्त्रीग्रहणं च ॥‖

(bb) वर्णग्रहणं च सर्वत्र ॥¶

(cc) प्रत्ययग्रहणं चापञ्चम्याः ॥

(dd) यस्मिन्विधिस्तदादावल्ग्रहणे ॥**

Patanjali shows, by giving the proper meaning of येन, *that Pâṇini's rule is not too widely applicable, and that it need not be changed to* प्रकृते तदन्तविधिः—

(a) raises an objection, which is refuted in (b).

(c, d) limit the rule.

(e) demands an additional rule; (f) shows how Pâṇini's rule might be altered so as not to necessitate the additional rule (e); (g) shows that in reality no additional rule is required. (h—cc) teach where and with what limitations or modifications to apply Pâṇini's rule.

Patanjali rejects (v) ; *he says that Pâṇini's rule is sufficient, or even preferable, if the statement* अलैवानर्थकेन नान्येनानर्थकेनेति वक्तव्यम्, *limited again by the other statement* अनिनस्मन्ग्रहणानि चार्थवता चानर्थकेन च तदन्तविधिं प्रयोजयन्ति, *be adopted.*

(dd) corrects Pâṇini's rule.

---

* Should be read twice in Benares edition and I. O. MS.

† MS. of I. O. प्रयोजनं महदप्स्वसृनप्तृणां दीर्घविधौ २.

‡ MS. of I. O. reads this twice.

§ MS. of I. O. सुपथिमथिपुंगोसखिचतुरनडुत्त्रिग्रहणं २ प्रयोजनम्.

‖ MS. of I. O. त्यदादिविधिभसादिस्त्रीग्रहणं च २ प्रयोजनम्.

¶ Should be read twice in Benares edition and I. O. MS.

** The Benares edition omits अल्ग्रहणेषु after वल्ग्रहणे.

Note.—*(p)* is called a Vârttika by Kaiyaṭa; *(a)*, *(g)*, *(h)*, *(v—x)*, *(bb)* and *(cc)* are called Vârttikas by Nâgojîbhaṭṭa, and *(a—d)*, *(h)*, *(i)*, *(l—s)*, and *(dd)*, by Bhaṭṭojidîkshita; Bhaṭṭoji also calls अलैषान्यर्थकेन a Vârttika. The Calcutta Edn. gives, not always correctly, (*c*), (*d*), (*e*), (*f*), (*h*), (*i*), (*n*—*t*) and (*v*).—Of the Paribhâshâs cited in it, (6) is a Vârttika (*dd*), (4) equivalent to Vârttika (*cc*), and (1) similar in purpose to what is stated in Vârttika (*g*); (5) and (7) are statements of Patanjali; (2) occurs in and (3) is based on Patanjali's remarks.

P. I, 1, 75—एङ् प्राचां देशे ||

No Vârttika.

Patanjali corrects Pâṇini's rule.

Note.—The Calcutta Edn. apparently mistakes Patanjali's correction for a Vârttika.

From the above it will appear that by adopting and practically applying the principle with which the first part of our enquiry had furnished us, we have been enabled to point out in Patanjali's discussions on 20 of Pâṇini's rules 135 Vârttikas; and I venture to hope that the reader who will examine the several Vârttikas appended to each of Pâṇini's rules, and compare the style and phraseology exhibited in all, and the manner in which Pâṇini's rules have been discussed in them, will grant that these Vârttikas bear the stamp of having been composed by one and the same author, and that taken together they form part of a work, complete in itself* and independent

* A very strong argument in favour of the assumption that Patanjali has recorded and commented on all the Vârttikas of Kâtyâyana, is furnished by the fact that whenever Kâtyâyana in such words as उक्तं or उक्तं वा refers to another of his Vârttikas, the Vârttika so instanced or referred to is invariably to be found in the Mahâbhâshya. The same argument holds good with regard to the Mahâbhâshya itself, and deserves perhaps some little consideration at the hands of those who maintain that the

of the rest of the Mahâbhâshya. Of this, at least, there can be no doubt, that the result at which we have arrived accords with the views held by the native grammarians. That these scholars have not made it their business to point out *all* the Vârttikas, but have told us only occasionally and incidentally that a particular statement was regarded by them as a Vârttika, has been mentioned already. I have also shown that out of the 135 statements which I have been led to consider as Vârttikas in the above, no less than 48 have actually been termed Vârttikas or ascribed to Kâtyâyana the Vârttikakâra, by Kaiyaṭa, Nâgojîbhaṭṭa, and Bhaṭṭojidîkshita, and it would be easy to prove that, if these 48 statements were regarded as Vârttikas by those grammarians, the same must necessarily have been the case with many more. On the other hand, to the best of my knowledge, the term Vârttika has, with two exceptions, never been applied to any of those remarks which I have considered as Patanjali's; and as regards those two exceptions, I feel no hesitation in saying that Bhaṭṭojidikshita has been in error; for both the statements which he terms Vârttikas, अपुरीति वक्तव्यम् on P. I, 1, 36, and अलैवानर्थकेन नान्येनानर्थकेनेति वक्तव्यम् on P. I, 1, 72, end with the phrase इति वक्तव्यम् which is foreign to the style of Kâtyâyana,* and in the case of the latter of those statements the context of the discussion in my opinion proves beyond doubt that it is Patanjali's.

IV.

Having fixed on a principle by which to distinguish in the Mahâbhâshya, as it has been handed down to us, between the

---

text of the Mahâbhâshya has been several times reconstructed out of fragments.

* Setting aside those cases in which Patanjali is commenting on Vârttikas, we find in the Mahâbhâshya on P. I, 1, altogether only 9 statements which end with वक्तव्यः or इति वक्तव्यम्. Of these, three, on P. I, 1, 36; 72; and 75 have been given already above. The remaining ones occur on P. I, 1, 1; 27; 57; 69; and 72; in them Patanjali states clearly the objections which are supposed to be refuted in particular Vârttikas; or he states objections which he refutes himself.

Vârttikas of Kâtyâyana and the original remarks of Patanjali, and having tested the worth of that principle by applying it practically for the reconstruction of a portion of the work of Kâtyâyana, we now recur to the question which led to this enquiry, the question as to the nature and the object of Kâtyâyana's Vârttikas, and of the work of Patanjali; and we may hope to answer that question the more readily and satisfactorily because we already have shown in the case of 20 of Pâṇini's rules, chosen at random, what is the tendency of Kâtyâyana's Vârttikas in regard to them, and what the relation of Patanjali in regard to those Vârttikas on the one hand and to the Sûtras of Pâṇini on the other. We begin with the Vârttikas of Kâtyâyana.

It is true that the Vârttikas are not a commentary on the rules of Pâṇini's grammar, and that it was not Kâtyâyana's intention to explain the meaning and the import of those rules, as they have been explained, *e.g.* by the author of the Kâśikâ Vṛitti. But it is in my opinion equally true that Kâtyâyana, in composing his Vârttikas, did *not* propose to himself the task of *finding fault* with Pâṇini; for he *justifies* the rules of his predecessor as often as he finds fault with them. So far from calling Kâtyâyana an unfair antagonist of Pâṇini, I would rather claim for him the title of a follower and judicious admirer of Pâṇini, who dispassionately examines the rules laid down by his master, considers the objections which have actually been or which might be raised to them, is ever ready to defend and justify Pâṇini, and corrects, adds to, or abandons the rules propounded by him, only when no other course is left open. It is true, Kâtyâyana states the objects of some of Pâṇini's rules in order to show that those objects are attained without those rules, and that the latter may therefore be dispensed with,—but he also explains to us the object and the purport of other rules in order either to show that those rules are not too widely applicable, or to obviate the objection that they are unnecessary. He states the objections to which the possible interpretations of a particular rule would be liable, but he also shows that those interpretations are nevertheless admissible, or suggests himself a correct interpretation. He discusses the several views that might be entertained regarding the objects of Pâṇini's rules, or their relation to other rules, and he states the objections to which those views would be open,—but in many instances he also refutes the objections advanced, and brings forward arguments in favour of one or more of the views propounded. He raises objections to whole rules or to particular terms employed in them, but he not seldom also proves those objections to be unfounded, and shows the correct way of applying a rule, or explains the import of a particular term, for the very purpose of meeting objections that might possibly be raised. If it cannot be denied that in many cases he corrects Pâṇini's rules, or suggests additional rules, it must also be admitted that there are many instances in which he proves that such corrections or additional rules are altogether uncalled for, or rendered unnecessary so soon as we adopt one or another maxim of interpretation the validity of which is proved by examples covering the whole range of Pâṇini's grammar. And if it is true on the one hand that some of Pâṇini's rules are declared by him unnecessary, it is on the other hand equally true that other rules which at first sight might seem to be unnecessary, are upheld by him and justified.

The object of the Vârttikas is then no other than this, without bias or prejudice to discuss such objections as might be raised to the rules of Pâṇini's grammar, and on the one hand to justify Pâṇini by defending him against unfounded criticism, and on the other hand to correct, reject, and add to, the rules laid down by him, where defence and justification were considered impossible. And this is in my opinion the true meaning of the definition of the term वार्त्तिक, as recorded by Nâgojibhaṭṭa, सूत्रे ऽनुक्तदुरुक्तचिन्ताकरत्वं वार्त्तिकत्वम्. The Vârttikas consider whether anything has been omitted in the Sûtras that should have been stated, and whether there is in them anything that is superfluous, faulty, or objectionable. A consideration of this nature would lead either to the justification of Pâṇini or to his condemnation, and

Kâtyâyana has given us ample proof that he has both justified and condemned the Sûtras of Pâṇini, the former perhaps even more than the latter. And from this point of view it will no longer be possible to question whether certain statements in the introductory Âhnika of the Mahâbhâshya have been correctly called Vârttikas by the native grammarians; for it must be patent to every one that the nature and object of those statements in no way differ from those of the rest of Kâtyâyana's Vârttikas. If it is admitted that the words and their meanings are fixed and settled by common usage, it may well be questioned whether the rules laid down by Pâṇini are at all necessary, and it must therefore be shown that and why they are necessary*; and if it is the object of grammar to lay down rules for the correct formation of those words which people actually use, it does not seem improper to enquire whether Pâṇini, in teaching the formation of such words as would not appear to be in use, has not laid himself open to just censure.† If, moreover, we are promised some transcendent benefit from the study of Pâṇini's grammar, we may well ask whether, to secure that benefit, it is sufficient for us to *know* the right words, as they have been taught by Pâṇini, or whether we only have to *employ* them.‡ It is also fair matter for discussion whether the name chosen for the science taught by Pâṇini is altogether appropriate and unobjectionable.§

---

* सिद्धे शब्दार्थसंबन्धे लोकतोऽर्थप्रयुक्ते शब्दप्रयोगे शास्त्रेण धर्मनियमो यथा लौकिकवैदिकेषु ॥

† अस्त्यप्रयुक्त इति चेन्नार्थे शब्दप्रयोगात्।
अप्रयोगः प्रयोगान्यत्वात्।
अप्रयुक्ते दीर्घसत्त्रवत्।
सर्वे देशान्तरे ॥

‡ ज्ञाने धर्म इति चेत्तथाधर्मः।
आचारे नियमः।
प्रयोगे सर्वलोकस्य।
शास्त्रपूर्वके प्रयोगेऽभ्युदयस्तत्तुल्यं वेदशब्देन ॥

§ सूत्रे व्याकरणे षष्ठ्यर्थोऽनुपपन्नः।
शब्दाप्रतिपत्तिः।
शब्दे ल्युडर्थः।
भवे प्रोक्तादयश्च तद्धिताः।
लक्ष्यलक्षणे व्याकरणम् ॥

And finally, when we are told that Pâṇini intended to teach the correct formation of words actually used, we may well raise the question why he should have commenced his grammar with an enumeration of the letters.*

Though I am obliged to differ from Prof. Goldstücker, I am not altogether at a loss to understand what may have led him to describe the nature and the object of the Vârttikas as he has done. The work which first brought the Sûtras of Pâṇini and the Vârttikas of Kâtyâyana within the range of the studies of European scholars, was the Calcutta Edition of Pâṇini. The editors of that work did not consider it necessary to append *all* the Vârttikas to their gloss; and unfortunately they in most cases selected those which contained objections and corrections, and omitted those others in which the corrections were rejected and the objections refuted † (see on P. I, 1, 1; 7; 12; 20; 22; 24; 26; 29, &c). Starting from such a selection of Vârttikas as they had given, it was not unnatural to arrive at the conclusion, which Prof. Goldstücker actually has arrived at, a conclusion which not even his subsequent profound knowledge of the Mahâbhâshya could induce him to modify.

We turn to Patanjali. That Patanjali has refuted some of the objections, that he has rejected some of the additional rules of Kâtyâyana, no student of the Mahâbhâshya would think of denying. But it is altogether contrary to fact to say that all the Vârttikas have been refuted by Patanjali, or to maintain that the Mahâbhâshya has been composed for the justification of Pâṇini. In proof of this assertion it would suffice to refer the reader to the analysis of part of the Mahâbhâshya which I have given above, and in which I have shown

---

* वृत्तिसमवायार्थ उपदेशः।
अनुबन्धकरणार्थश्च।
इष्टबुद्ध्यर्थश्चेति चेदुदात्तानुदात्तस्वरितानुनासिकदीर्घप्लुतानामप्युपदेशः।
आकृत्युपदेशात्सिद्धमिति चेत्संवृतादीनां प्रतिषेधः॥

† To use two terms which have been employed, *e.g.* by Bhaṭṭojidikshita on P. I, 1, 10, the Calcutta editors have given us the *Pûrvapaksha*-vârttikas, but they have omitted the *Siddhânta*-vârttikas.

that more than half of the 135 Vârttikas pointed out have been unreservedly adopted by Patanjali; but I will try to corroborate it by additional evidence. I have stated already that whereas in the case of P. I, 1, 6 Kâtyâyana only objects to the words दीधीवेवी of that rule, Patanjali proves the whole rule to be superfluous; and that while Kâtyâyana defends P. I, 1, 36 from an objection, his defence is not accepted, and Pâṇini's rule altered, by Patanjali. I have also shown that Patanjali declares the डति either of P. 1, 1, 23 or 25 to be superfluous, and that he rejects the rule I, 1, 49, which had been justified by Kâtyâyana, in the sense ordinarily ascribed to it, altogether. Similarly, while Kâtyâyana thinks it right to defend P. I, 1, 8 from a possible objection, Patanjali rejects the word मुख from that rule; and while Kâtyâyana on P. I, 1, 41 enumerates three cases as the only ones for which it would be necessary to term an Avyayîbhâva Avyaya, Patanjali rejects the rule altogether. In the same way Patanjali refutes a Vârttika on P. I, 1, 56 which shows the purport of that rule, and he tries to prove that Pâṇini's rule may be dispensed with; and he shows on P. I, 1, 62 that either the प्रत्ययस्य of the preceding rule or the first प्रत्यय of I, 1, 62 may be omitted. Such a proceeding cannot be called *justifying* Pâṇini.

The Mahâbhâshya is in the first instance a *commentary on Kâtyâyana's Vârttikas.* This must be evident from all I have had occasion to state in the first part of this enquiry, and this too is the view entertained by the native grammarians. Puṇyarâja informs us that Patanjali composed his work वार्त्तिकव्याख्यानपुरःसरम्, and Jinendrabuddhi, when commenting on the word भाष्ये in the introductory verse of the Kâsikâ-vṛitti, tells us distinctly भाष्यं कात्यायनप्रणीतानां वाक्यानां पतञ्जलिप्रणीतम्.

But Patanjali did not rest satisfied with being a mere commentator. Having started as a commentator, he became a follower and imitator of the man whose work he was explaining. He unreservedly adopted Kâtyâyana's method of discussing the Sûtras of Pâṇini, and like most imitators carried that method to extremes. Finding that Kâtyâyana had left unnoticed certain Sûtras of Pâṇini which were or which might appear to be liable to objection, he drew those rules within the range of his discussion, and either refuted the objections to which they seemed to be open, or showed that Pâṇini was really in the wrong and that his rules ought to be corrected. Or finding that Kâtyâyana had failed to notice objections to rules which *had* been discussed by him, he thought it necessary to do what had been left undone by his master. On the other hand, not approving of the way in which certain objections had been met by Kâtyâyana, or finding that the objections refuted by the latter admitted of different refutations, he either substituted his own refutations for those of Kâtyâyana, or strengthened the views held by that scholar by additional arguments of his own. Again, believing himself to be in the possession of arguments by which to refute objections to Pâṇini's rules which had been stated by Kâtyâyana, but which the latter had been unable to refute, or by which to prove the uselessness of corrections or additional rules which Kâtyâyana had thought fit to adopt, he employed those arguments to refute those objections, corrections, and additional rules, and in doing so he refuted the Vârttikas of Kâtyâyana. On the other hand, there are not wanting instances in which he proved his superior skill by showing that Kâtyâyana had done wrong in defending Pâṇini, and by supporting the very objection which Kâtyâyana had laboured to refute. If by adopting such a course of procedure Patanjali has defended Pâṇini from some of the objections brought against him by Kâtyâyana, it is on the other hand equally true that in many cases his criticism is much more thorough-going and destructive than Kâtyâyana's, and that Pâṇini has suffered more at *his* hands than at those of the Vârttikakâra.*

---

* Where there is a difference of opinion between Pâṇini and Kâtyâyana, or between Kâtyâyana and Patanjali, or between all the three, the native grammarians attach a higher value to the views of Kâtyâyana than to those of Pâṇini, and a higher value again to those of Patanjali than to those either of Kâtyâyana or of Pâṇini. That such should be the case is not unnatural, and it might appear unnecessary to allude to it here, were it not that Prof. Weber has expressed a somewhat different view when discussing the meaning of the word *Âchâryadeśîya* (Ind. Stud. XIII,

The object which Kâtyâyana and Patanjali have in view throughout their works, is one and the same; the nature of their remarks on Pâṇini's rules is identically one; both differ in the form which they have given to their discussions and in the extent to which they have carried them, and to which they have availed themselves of such artifices as *Nipâtana, Jnâpaka, &c.* Were we to omit the text of the Vârttikas and to retain only Patanjali's explanations of them, or were we to

---

page 317). Prof. Goldstücker was of opinion that this word denoted Patanjali as the countryman of the Âchârya, understanding by *Âchârya* Kâtyâyana. Prof. Bhâṇḍarkar had referred it likewise to Patanjali, but had understood it to mean 'Âchârya the younger.' Prof. Weber, without actually refuting these two interpretations, is apparently inclined to take the word, in accordance with Pâṇini's rules, in the sense of 'an unaccomplished teacher,' and he disposes of the objection that Kaiyaṭa, who uses the word Âchâryadeśîya, would not have called Patanjali an unaccomplished teacher, by stating, that since Kaiyaṭa once has placed the Vârttikakâra even above the Sûtrakâra, it would seem even less strange that he should have placed the same Vârttikakâra also above Patanjali, 'although it would appear curious enough that he should have spoken of Patanjali in *so* disparaging a manner.' Here Prof. Weber appears to have overlooked the fact that Kaiyaṭa in another place of his work has distinctly told us his views as to the relative value of the teachings of Pâṇini, Kâtyâyana, and Patanjali. For when commenting on a passage of the Mahâbhâshya on P. I, 1, 29, Kaiyaṭa lays down the well-known maxim यथोत्तरंमुनित्रयस्य प्रामाण्यम्. 'the later the Muni, the greater his authority;' Kâtyâyana is a higher authority than Pâṇini, and Patanjali a higher authority than Kâtyâyana or Pâṇini.

The word *Âchâryadeśîya* does mean 'an unaccomplished teacher,' and it is opposed to *Âchârya;* but it is not synonymous with Patanjali, nor does the word *Âchârya* necessarily denote Kâtyâyana. Those who are acquainted with the method followed in the Mahâbhâshya, must be aware that in many cases Patanjali does not at once acquaint us with the final and correct view (*Siddhânta*) on the matter under discussion, but leads up to it by degrees. While doing so, he not seldom propounds views which contain a part of the truth, but which, as they contain truth mixed with error, are subsequently abandoned in favour of the *Siddhânta*. And in these cases it is customary with the commentators to consider those views which are partly correct and partly incorrect, as views of an *Âchâryadeśîya*, a disputant who has some idea of the true state of the case but does not know the whole truth, and to contrast with them the views of the

translate Patanjali's original remarks into the language of Kâtyâyana, we should find it an exceedingly hard task, a task in most cases altogether impossible of solution, to distinguish between the two grammarians. Of this fact the native commentators were well aware, and hence discussions such as those of Nâgojîbhaṭṭa on P. I, 1, 12, as to whether Patanjali is giving his own remarks, or is commenting on Vârttikas which have been omitted in the MSS.*

It is not seldom that in the works of European scholars we meet with the statement that Patanjali has commented on and explained the rules of Pâṇini; but that statement can be accepted as true only if a meaning be assigned to the words

---

Âchârya, the disputant whose views are entirely correct and finally adopted. They in fact employ the two terms in the same manner in which they also use the words *Siddhântyekadeśin* and *Siddhântin*. Where Patanjali leads up to a *Vârttika* which is finally adopted by him, by stating a view which is only partly correct, the view to which he thus gives expression, is the view of an *Âchâryadeśîya*, and the view taken in the Vârttika that of the *Âchârya*. But where the two views, as happens to be the case not unfrequently, are *both* propounded by Patanjali, Patanjali himself is both the *Âchâryadeśîya* and also the *Âchârya*. When commenting on the Vârttika पद्युष्मदस्मद्° on P. I, 1, 72, Patanjali raises the question whether the word पद् of that Vârt. is an instance for पदाधिकारे or अङ्गाधिकारे in the preceding Vârt. पदाङ्गाधिकारे°. In the words एवं तर्ह्यङ्गाधिकारे प्रयोजनं नास्तीति° he first states the view that it is an instance for पदाधिकारे; but that view he afterwards abandons in favour of the correct view that पद् is an instance for अङ्गाधिकारे. In this case there is no question between a view of Patanjali's and one of Kâtyâyana's; both views are propounded by Patanjali. And yet Nâgojîbhaṭṭa contrasts the two views with each other, by calling the view first stated that of the *Âchâryadeśîya*. It is the view of an Âchâryadeśiya, because it is partly correct and partly incorrect; पद् *is* an instance for the Vârttika पदाङ्गाधिकारे, but it is an instance for the term अङ्गाधिकारे of that Vârttika, and *not* for पदाधिकारे. See also for a similar example Kaiyaṭa on P. IV, 1, 162.

* The question on P. I, 1, 12 is, whether in the words अथवा प्रत्ययसंज्ञा°—मार्थादीदाद्यर्थानामिति (on page 79*a* of the Benares Edition) Pantanjali is giving his own arguments or is commenting on the three Vârttikas वचनसामर्थ्याद्वा । योगविभागाद्वा ॥ मार्थादीदाद्यर्थानां वा ॥ omitted in the MSS. (कोशे).

explanation and comment, which those words do not convey generally. For, so far as my own experience goes, Patanjali never tells us the import of a whole rule or of a particular term of a rule, he never quotes instances or counterinstances, for the simple purpose of explanation, but always does so either to show that such rule is absolutely necessary, and that the objects for which it has been given are not attained by other rules, in other words, to justify Pâṇini; or he does so for the purpose of showing subsequently that such rule or part of a rule is not necessary, and that it therefore may be dispensed with. The *Bhâshya*kâra, in short, is not a *Vṛitti*kâra, and the functions of both are carefully kept separate by the commentators. When Patanjali on P. I, 1, 4 asks why Pâṇini has employed the terms धातु and आर्धधातुके in his rule, and when he quotes counterinstances, apparently to explain the meaning and import of those terms, Kaiyaṭa shows us the real purpose of Patanjali's proceeding by saying क्रमेण सूत्रप्रत्याख्यानायार्धधातुकस्य च लोपविशेषणत्वे धातुग्रहणानर्थक्यप्रतिपादनाय प्रत्युदाहरणोपन्यासः, and Nâgojîbhaṭṭa justifies Kaiyaṭa's remark by adding ननु पदप्रयोजनचिन्ता वृत्तिकारस्योचिता न भाष्यकारस्येत्यत आह क्रमेणेति। तत्तत्पदप्रयोजनखण्डनक्रमेणेत्यर्थः ॥ And when Patanjali on P. I, 1, 57 asks why Pâṇini has employed the term अचः in his rule, and when in answer to that question he quotes a number of counterinstances which by the term अचः would seem to be excluded from Pâṇini's rule, Kaiyaṭa again considers the occasion worthy of remark and tells us that the question has been raised (not to explain Pâṇini's rule, but) to show that for *some* of the Pratyudâharaṇas which are given in the commentaries, the term अचः would be unnecessary ('वार्त्तानि प्रत्युदाहरणानि कानिचिच्छक्यपरिविधानानीति प्रश्नो ऽच इति किमिति.'), and Nâgojibhaṭṭa again appends to Kaiyaṭa's remark the explanatory statement प्रत्युदाहरणादिचिन्ता वृत्तिकाराणामुचिता न तु भाष्यकृतो ऽत आह वार्त्तानीति. When on P. I, 1, 50 Patanjali asks for an example of that rule, Kaiyaṭa shows the reason for that question by saying क्वचिल्लक्षणान्तरेणेष्टं सिद्धमिति प्रश्नः; and when Patanjali on I, 1, 56 enquires why Pâṇini has employed the term स्थानिवत् instead of saying merely स्थानी, Kaiyaṭa informs us of the real import of Patanjali's question by stating विनापि वर्तिना तदर्थलाभो यथा स्यादिति भावः. Nowhere does Patanjali explain Pâṇini for the simple purpose of explanation, but like a second Vârttikakâra, he enquires whether anything has been omitted in the Sûtras that should have been stated, or whether in them there is anything superfluous, faulty, or at all liable to objection.

Here I conclude. To show in detail the differences between Kâtyâyana and Patanjali would be a task full of interest, and highly instructive, as showing the progress which the science of grammar had undoubtedly made from the time of Kâtyâyana to that of Patanjali, and as tracing in the work of the latter the germs of those failings which have continued growing and increasing in the works of the later grammarians ever since. But that task does not lie within the scope of this enquiry, nor would the materials at my command justify my undertaking it at present. My purpose is attained if in future it will be impossible to stigmatize Kâtyâyana as an *unfair antagonist* of Pâṇini, and to speak of Patanjali as *refuting* the Vârttikas of Kâtyâyana, or *justifying* Pâṇini.

APPENDIX.

In order to enable the reader to judge for himself of the value of the *Vârttikapâṭha* which I have mentioned on page 6, I publish below the first chapter of that work from the MS. in my possession.

सिद्धे शब्दार्थसंबन्धे लोकतोऽर्थप्रयुक्ते शब्दप्रयोगे शास्त्रेण धर्मनियमो यथा लौकिकवैदिकेषु । समानायामर्थावगतौ शब्देन चापशब्देन च शब्देनैवार्थोऽभिधेय इति नियमः ॥

तत्र ज्ञानपूर्वके प्रयोगे धर्मः ॥

न चेदानीमाचार्याः सूत्राणि कृत्वा निवर्तयन्ति ॥

वृत्तिसमवायार्थोऽनुबन्धकरणार्थश्च वर्णानामुपदेशः । शास्त्रप्रवृत्तिफलको वर्णानां क्रमेण निवेशो वृत्तिसमवायः ॥

अ इ उण् ॥

आकृतिग्रहणात्सिद्धम् । रूपसामान्याद्वा ॥

ऋ ऌक् ॥

समाने चार्थे शास्त्रान्वितोऽशास्त्रान्वितस्य निवर्तको भवति । एवं समाने शब्दे शास्त्रान्वितोऽप्यर्थोऽस्य निवर्तको भवति तुल्यन्यायात् ॥

पक्षान्तरैरपि परिहारा भवन्ति ॥

ए ओङ् ॥

वर्णैकदेशा वर्णग्रहणेन गृह्यन्ते ॥

नाव्यपवृक्तस्यावयवस्य तद्विधिः ॥

अथवा न गृह्यन्ते ॥

ह य व र ट् ॥

रेफस्यानुनासिकपरसवर्णप्रतिषेधो वक्तव्यः ॥

रेफोष्मणां सवर्णा न सन्ति ॥

नेमौ रहौ कार्यिणाविति च ॥

अयोगवाहानामट्सूपदेशः कार्यः । शर्षु च ॥

अर्थवन्तो वर्णा धात्वादीनामेकवर्णानामर्थदर्शनात् ॥

अनर्थकास्तु प्रतिवर्णमर्थानुपलब्धेः ॥

तत्र स्वभावाद्धात्वादय एकवर्णा अर्थवन्तोऽन्येऽनर्थका इति तत्त्वम् ॥

प्रत्याहारेऽनुबन्धानां कथमज्ग्रहणेषु न ।

आचारादप्रधानत्वाल्लोपश्च बलवत्तरः ॥

अक्षरं न क्षरं विद्यादश्नोतेर्वा सरोऽक्षरम् ।

वर्णं वाहुः पूर्वसूत्रे किमर्थमुपदिश्यते ॥

वर्णज्ञानं वाग्विषयो यत्र च ब्रह्म वर्तते ।

तदर्थमिष्टबुद्ध्यर्थं लघ्वर्थं चोपदिश्यते ॥

वृद्धिरादैच् ॥ १॥

छन्दोवत्सूत्राणि भवन्ति । छन्दोवत्कवयः कुर्वन्तीति नेष्टिः ॥

अथ संज्ञेति वक्तव्यम् ॥

आचार्यव्यवहारात्संज्ञात्वसिद्धिः ॥

पूर्वोच्चारितः संज्ञी परोच्चारिता संज्ञा ॥

सतो हि कार्यिणः कार्येण भवितव्यम् ॥

मङ्गलादीनि शास्त्राणि प्रथन्ते वीरपुरुषाणि च भवन्त्यायुष्मत्पुरुषाणि चाध्येतारश्च वृद्धियुक्ता भवन्ति ॥

इतरेतराश्रयाणि च कार्याणि न प्रकल्पन्ते ॥

प्रत्येकं वाक्यपरिसमाप्तिः । समुदाये वाक्यपरिसमाप्तिः ॥

गुणा भेदकाः । अभेदकाश्च । तत्राभेदका इत्येव न्याय्यम् ॥

तकारः मुखसुखोच्चारणार्थः ॥

इको गुणवृद्धी ॥ ३ ॥

यं विधिं प्रत्युपदेशोऽनर्थकः स विधिर्बाध्यते यस्य तु विधेर्निमित्तमेव नासौ बाध्यते ॥

मण्डूकगतयोऽधिकाराः ॥

न धातुलोप आर्धधातुके ॥ ४ ॥

प्रसक्तस्यानभिनिर्वृत्तस्य प्रतिषेधेन निवृत्तिः ॥

(दीधीवेवीटाम् ॥ ६ ॥)

दृष्टानुविधिश्छन्दसि ॥

हलोऽनन्तराः संयोगः ॥ ७ ॥

अतज्जातीयव्यवाये नानन्तर्यम् ॥

तुल्यास्यप्रयत्नं सवर्णम् ॥ ९ ॥

ऋकारल्कारयोः सवर्णसंज्ञा विधेया ॥

उरण् रपर इत्यत्र लपरत्वं वक्तव्यम् ॥

अदसो मात् ॥ १२ ॥

नैकं प्रयोजनं योगारम्भं प्रयोजयति ॥

निपात एकाजनाङ् ॥१४ ॥

ईषदर्थे क्रियायोगे मर्यादाभिविधौ च यः ।

एतमातं ङितं विद्याद्वाक्यस्मरणयोरङित् ॥

तरप्तमपौ घः ॥ २२ ॥

इह व्याकरणे सर्वेष्वेव सानुबन्धकग्रहणेषु रूपमाश्रीयते यत्रास्यैतद्रूपमिति रूपनिर्ग्रहश्च नान्तरेण लौकिकं प्रयोगं तस्मिंश्च लौकिके प्रयोगे सानुबन्धकानां प्रयोगो नास्तीति कृत्वा द्वितीयः प्रयोग उपास्यत उपदेशो नाम ॥

बहुगणवतुडति संख्या ॥ २३ ॥

कृत्रिमाकृत्रिमयोः कृत्रिमे कार्यसंप्रत्ययः ॥

अप्रकरणज्ञं प्रति गोपालकमानयेत्युक्त उभयगतिस्तस्य भवति । साधीयो यष्टिहस्तं गमिष्यति ॥

अध्यर्धशब्दस्य संख्यासंज्ञा वक्तव्या समासकन्विध्यर्थम् । लुकि चाग्रहणम् ॥

अर्धपूर्वपदश्च पूरणप्रत्ययान्तः संख्यासंज्ञ इति वक्तव्यं समासकन्विध्यर्थम् ॥

अधिकग्रहणं चालुकि समासोत्तरपदवृद्ध्यर्थम् । बहुव्रीहौ चाग्रहणम् ॥

ष्णान्ता षट् ॥ २४ ॥

उपदेशे ष्णान्तेति वक्तव्यम् । न वा ॥

यथालक्षणमप्रयुक्ते । तत्र लक्षणाभावस्य योग्यतेत्यर्थः ॥

क्तक्तवतू निष्ठा ॥ २६ ॥

अनुबन्धो लुप्तोऽपि कालकारकादिविशेषानुपलक्षयति ॥

सर्वादीनि सर्वनामानि ॥ २७ ॥

बहुव्रीहौ तद्गुणसंविज्ञानमपि ॥

बाधकान्येव निपातनानि ॥

संज्ञोपसर्जनीभूतानां पाठात्पर्युदासो वक्तव्यः ॥

अङ्गाधिकारे यदुच्यते गृह्यमाणविभक्तेस्तद्भवति । सप्तमीनिर्दिष्टे यदुच्यते प्रकृतविभक्तौ तद्भवति ॥

अन्तरं बहिर्योगोपसंव्यानयोः ॥ ३६ ॥

अपुरीति वक्तव्यम् ॥

थाप्रकरणे तीयस्य ङित्सूपसंख्यानम् । विभाषा द्वितीयेत्यादि न कर्तव्यम् ॥

तद्धितश्चासर्वविभक्तिः ॥ ३८ ॥

एवं गते कृत्यपि तुल्यमेतन्मान्तस्य कार्यं ग्रहणं न तत्र ।
ततः परे चाभिमता न कार्यास्त्रयः कृदर्था ग्रहणेन योगाः ॥
कृत्तद्धितानां ग्रहणं तु कार्यं संख्याविशेषं ह्यभिनिश्रिता ये ।
तस्मात्स्वरादिग्रहणं च कार्यं कृत्तद्धितानां ग्रहणं च पाठे ॥
सदृशं त्रिषु लिङ्गेष्वित्यादि च ॥

कृन्मेजन्तः ॥ ३९ ॥

अनन्यप्रकृतिरिति वाच्यम् । न वा संनिपातलक्षणेत्यादि ॥

अव्ययीभावश्च ॥ ४१ ॥

लुग्मुखस्वरोपचाराः प्रयोजनमिति परिगणनं कर्तव्यम् ॥

मिदचोऽन्त्यात्परः ॥ ४७ ॥

नैवेश्वर आज्ञापयति नापि धर्मसूत्रकाराः पठन्त्यसंभवेऽपवादैरुत्सर्गा बाध्यन्तामिति । किं तर्हि । लौकिको दृष्टान्तः । लोके हि सत्यपि संभवे बाधनं भवति । यथा दधि ब्राह्मणेभ्य इत्यादौ सत्यपि संभवे तक्रदानं दधिदानस्य निवर्तकं भवति ॥

अन्त्यात्पूर्वो मस्जेरनुषङ्गसंयोगादिलोपार्थमिति वक्तव्यम् ॥

भर्जिमस्जोरन्त्यात्पूर्वो वक्तव्यः ॥

एच इग्घ्रस्वादेशे ॥ ४८ ॥

सिद्धमेङः सस्थानत्वादेचोश्चोत्तरभूयस्त्वादिति ॥

षष्ठी स्थानेयोगा ॥ ४९ ॥

अधिकारश्च त्रिप्रकारकः। कश्चिदेकदेशस्थः सर्वं शास्त्रमभिज्वलयति प्रदीपवत्। अपरो यथा रज्ज्वा बद्धं काष्ठमनुकृष्यते तद्वदनुकृष्यते चकारेण। अपरः प्रतियोगं तस्यानिर्देशार्थ इति योगे योग उपतिष्ठते॥

स्थानिवदादेशोऽनल्विधौ ॥ ५६ ॥

सामान्यातिदेशे विशेषानतिदेशः॥

एकदेशविकृतस्योपसंख्यानम्। लोकन्यायात्सिद्धमेतन्न हि श्वा पुच्छे छिन्ने गर्दभो भवति॥

स्थानी नाम यो भूत्वा नो भवत्यादेशो नाम यो ऽभूत्वा भवति॥

बुद्धिविपरिणाममात्रं वा॥

तयादेश उभयप्रतिषेधो वक्तव्यः। विप्रतिषेधात्सिद्धम्॥

त्रयादेशे स्रन्तस्य प्रतिषेधो वक्तव्यः। विप्रतिषेधाद्वा॥

आम्विधौ च स्रन्तस्य प्रतिषेधो वक्तव्यः। विप्रतिषेधाद्वा॥

स्वरे वंस्वादेशे प्रतिषेधो वक्तव्यः॥

गोः पूर्वणित्त्वात्वस्वरेषु प्रतिषेधो वक्तव्यः॥

न पदान्त० ॥ ५८ ॥

स्वरदीर्घयलोपेषु लोपाजादेश एव न स्थानिवदिति वक्तव्यम्॥

क्विलुगुपधात्वचङ्परनिर्ह्रासेषूपसंख्यानम्॥

पूर्वत्रासिद्धे न स्थानिवदिति वक्तव्यम्॥

वरेयलोपस्वरवर्जं द्विर्वचनादीनि च न कर्तव्यानि॥

तस्य दोषः संयोगादिलोपलत्वणत्वेष्विति वक्तव्यम्॥